GETTING BACK UP

How Mercy Forgives and Grace Restores

DR. DAVID HARPOOL

WESTBOW
PRESS®
A DIVISION OF THOMAS NELSON
& ZONDERVAN

THE HOLY BIBLE, NEW INTERNATIONAL VERSION®, NIV® Copyright © 1973, 1978, 1984, 2011 by Biblica, Inc.® Used by permission. All rights reserved worldwide.

WestBow Press books may be ordered through booksellers or by contacting:

WestBow Press
A Division of Thomas Nelson & Zondervan
1663 Liberty Drive
Bloomington, IN 47403
www.westbowpress.com
1 (866) 928-1240

ISBN: 978-1-5127-9883-8 (sc)
ISBN: 978-1-5127-9884-5 (hc)
ISBN: 978-1-5127-9882-1 (e)

Library of Congress Control Number: 2017912459

Print information available on the last page.

WestBow Press rev. date: 08/30/2017

Special thanks to:

- Reverend Dr. Paul and Betty Swadley, who taught me most of the concepts in this book.
- Bob and Connie Bilyeu, who lived the concepts of this book in front of me.
- Jack and Winnie Tuckness, Richard and Barbara Woods, Rod Kissenger, Scott, Lonnie and Mark Killingsworth, and Dr. Jim Joslin, who invested time in my life when they didn't have to.
- Mom, Dad, and my brothers, who gave me and taught me unconditional love.
- Amy, Samantha, Zach, and Caleb, who have shown me mercy and grace as I've tried to be a husband and father.
- Young Life, who shares these concepts with hundreds of thousands of kids.
- Chris, John, Charlie, and Jerry, who were there at the falls and still loved me.
- To those who attended the churches I have served for making me want to know more about the God of mercy and grace.
- South Haven Baptist Church, my childhood retreat.
- Johanna Randle, for editing the original version of this book.
- First American Baptist Church of Longmont, for all your support.

CONTENTS

CHAPTER 1

MERCY AND GRACE
ARE FOR MESSES

If you are reading this, then you or someone you know (or perhaps many people you know) have taken what I call, "the fall." You may be or may want to minister to people who have hit the bottom. Simply stated, the fall is when our lives get off-track. Some falls are minor, and others are full-fledged derailments. The fall is often in the eyes of the beholder. The closer you are to God, the less it takes the fall to have devastating results.

Unfortunately, Billy Joel was right when he sang, "I'd rather laugh with the sinners than cry with the saints. The sinners are much more fun." The problem is that the *fun,* isn't fun, when it moves us off the plan God has for us. The real world is fallen, and as such, we hurt, make mistakes, hurt others, are lonely, depressed, cynical, and narcissistic—and we have scars to prove it. Jesus did what he did, not because we are perfect, but because he knew at one time or another, we are all messes. Jesus knew we would take the fall.

Philip Yancey, in his book *What's So Amazing About Grace?* accurately describes this phenomenon:

> Having spent time around "sinners" and around purported saints, I have a hunch why Jesus spent so much time with the former group: I think he preferred their company. Because the sinners were honest about themselves and had no pretense, Jesus could deal with them. In contrast, the saints put on airs, judged him, and sought to catch him in a moral trap. In the end, it was the saints, not the sinners, who arrested Jesus.

FALL FROM GRACE

There is a horrible saying we use in our society, especially in our culture, that isn't biblical (with one exception), and it's the opposite of what Jesus did and taught. This is the concept that someone has had a "fall from grace." You and I can't fall from grace. We can only choose to walk away from grace or not to accept it.

In his book *God is With You Every Day,* Max Lucado writes:

> The wasted years of life. The poor choices of life. God answers the mess of life with one word: grace! Grace. We know the word. The bank gives us a grace period. Grace shares the church parsonage with its cousins: forgiveness, faith,

and fellowship. But do we really understand it? We've settled for wimpy grace. It politely occupies a phrase in a hymn and fits nicely on a church sign. Have you been changed by grace? Shaped by grace? Strengthened by grace? Softened by grace? God's grace has a drenching about it. A wildness about it. Grace comes after you! From insecure to God-secure. From afraid-to-die to ready-to-fly. Grace is the word that calls us to change and then gives us the power to pull it off!

But sometimes it isn't easy to accept grace. It has been observed that God will use whatever he needs to use, to get our attention. Sometimes we face mountains, deserts, stormy seas, health crises, relationship disasters, and employment problems, and God uses those circumstances to remind us that, above all else, we need him.

Sometimes it takes a fall, or a series of them, for God to get ahold of us. For me, the fall has been a series of falls. Some were absolutely my fault, and I own them. One was a sin followed by more bad decisions. Others were just the consequences of living in a fallen world. Some of my falls were literally a lost job, a flood, a tornado, a fire, and a spinal-cord injury, but as the song said, they "got a hold of me." That might give you a picture of my stubbornness. In fact, all of those things actually happened while I was getting up off the bottom and trying to find my way back to faith. You may relate even more to a song written by Jimmy Yeary, Rebecca Bowman, and Sonya Isaacs, entitled "Why Can We?" It states, "He just can't forgive himself and forget, even though God already did." Most of the massive falls in the Bible happened to people who had begun to think they were all-powerful and who were self-absorbed. However, God still wanted and did use many of them to do great things.

That's the purpose of this book. I'm tired of good people who've made mistakes being thrown on the human waste pile. I'm tired of scores of good husbands, wives, teachers, students, builders, group leaders, and pastors who have made mistakes being turned into outcasts in the name of God. I'm tired of meeting people who just can't forgive themselves or someone else and have surrendered to anger and their worst common denominator. I assure you; God hasn't abandoned you or given up on his plan for your life.

GOD HAS NOT ABANDONED YOU, NO MATTER WHAT YOU'VE DONE!

The promise that God will never leave you may seem impossible to believe depending on where you are in the fall. However, either God can be trusted or he can't. We don't get to choose to *kind of* trust him. God claims to be trustworthy no matter the circumstance. He claims to be trustworthy no matter what you've done. God has made these promises:

- "Be strong and courageous. Do not be afraid or terrified because of them, for the LORD your God goes with you;

he will never leave you nor forsake you" (Deuteronomy 31:6; my emphasis).

- "The LORD himself goes before you and will be with you; he will never leave you nor forsake you. *Do not be afraid; do not be discouraged*" (Deuteronomy 31:8; my emphasis).
- "No one will be able to stand up against you all the days of your life. *As I was with Moses, so I will be with you*" (Joshua 1:5; my emphasis).
- "I will turn the darkness into light before them and make the rough places smooth. These are the things I will do; *I will not forsake them*" (Isaiah 42:16; my emphasis).

God has clearly said that he is trustworthy and that he will not abandon us. It is up to you and me to hold God accountable for that promise and trust him.

THE BAD GOSPEL

I know I am not supposed to call a gospel bad, but some churches preach a bad gospel. Some churches preach condemnation and judgment. After listening to their message, you are convinced that God is mad at you—that he hates you and is looking for a reason to punish you. That is a bad gospel. It isn't really even the gospel. The gospel is good news. If you have been a victim of the *bad gospel*, forget what they told you and know that no matter what you've done, God loves you. He loves you *so much* (the ignored words of John 3:16) that he gave his only son as a substitute to pay for every bad thing you've ever done or ever will do. That is the real gospel.

I heard a pastor once say, "Why is it that the church spends so much time talking about what the Bible says so little about, and so little time talking about what the Bible says so much about?" I couldn't agree more. That's why this book is about God's greatest attribute: love. The way he chooses to love us is through mercy (forgiveness) and grace (restoration). I am not asking you to make a single change in the way you live—yet. But it is time to quit lying to yourself.

You Won't Change on Your Own

We lie to ourselves and say we can keep on doing exactly what we've been doing and eventually things will get better. They won't. If you could solve your situation, you would have already done it. I spent at least ten years telling myself that my way of doing it would eventually work. It didn't. There is a story in the Bible (John, Chapter 5) where a man had been laying on the ground and lying to himself for thirty-eight years. He told himself, "If I just keep repeating what I'm doing, sooner or later it will get better." It didn't. Jesus approached the man, and before saying "Take your mat, get up, and walk," he asked the man, "Do you want to get well?" In an older translation, it reads, "Wilt thou be made whole?"

I've never met anyone who didn't really want to be well or made whole. However, I've met a lot of people who want to get well and become whole on their own terms and conditions. What is your condition for you to accept mercy that forgives and grace that restores? Are you someone who wants to be well and get whole … *if*?

- If it doesn't require the hard work of acknowledging the mistakes and making the required changes.
- If you can get it all back—everything you've lost. You want to be restored to the day before the fall. You want the life you had—not the one God has for you after mercy forgives and grace restores.
- If the perpetrator of your harm suffers first and you're not required to forgive.
- If you don't have to deal with what others will think or say.
- If you can keep drinking too much, cheating when it feels good, and stealing—even though work is harder.
- If you can keep the focus on yourself and on what you want and not on what God has planned for you.

You and I are not alone or unique in wanting to set terms and conditions for our comeback. Moses asked God to find someone else. Jonah was willing to go, just not to Nineveh. Thomas wanted to believe but needed to first touch the scars of Jesus. To experience the mercy that forgives and the grace that restores, we have to approach God on his terms, not our conditions. Following our terms is what got us in trouble in the first place.

WHY WE NEED GOD-VISION

One of the traps we fall into is that we begin to lose perspective, and as we lose perspective, we lose accuracy in our vision. Not physical vision, but our ability to see things as they are.

We begin to see only the bad in us, as if we somehow surprised God by being fallen, broken repeat offenders (sinners). That makes us focus on who we are by nature and not what we can become through Jesus. We stare at our failure list and think that what we see defines us. It doesn't.

We begin to see only our circumstances, which are likely awful before, during and after the fall. We can't see God in all his power and ability to fix what's broken because our vision is tunnel, limited, and blind.

Those around us also lack God-vision. They see only our mistakes, our brokenness, and the mess we've made of our lives. Jesus noted our blindness when we judge others when he said, "Why do you look at the speck of sawdust in your brother's eye and pay no attention to the plank in your own eye?" (Matthew 7:3). Grace-deniers especially suffer from a lack of God-vision. It's hard to see with a 2x4 in your eyes and self-righteousness in your heart. Ask Jesus: it was the blind religious and the powerful political leaders who killed him.

HOW DOES GOD SEE US?

God has God-vision; he sees us with the potential of creation. He sees us as becoming what he created us to be. When we ask for forgiveness, he doesn't see our mistakes, messes, and a giant disappointment. He sees us as clean slates that can become the creations he had in mind when he created us. He sees us as his children. Jesus says to us, "You didn't earn my love and thus you can't lose it." He says, "Open your eyes and see that I so loved you that I died for you." He declares your past has nothing to do with your future in Christ.

You're saying, "Yeah, maybe once I had the potential to be all he wanted me to be, but not now, not after the fall." How arrogant of you and me. We see (with our limited vision) God as being so small that we—just one tiny, minuscule part of his creation—can thwart his purpose and will. Ephesians reminds us of how arrogant this thinking is. "In him we were also chosen, having been predestined according to the plan of him who works out everything in conformity with the purpose of his will" (1:11).

"Who works out everything" for his purpose. Read it this way: "He created us, has a plan for us based in love, and will overcome our messes, mistakes, colossal failures, and falls … to make it work out for the purpose he created for us." It is not about what we did, it is about what Jesus has already done.

We aren't so big and bad that we can stop the God of the universe from working his plan. God says, "Relax, get over yourself, ask for forgiveness, and embrace restoring grace. I've got this."

CHAPTER 2

HERE IN THE REAL WORLD, PEOPLE FALL

This poem describes that point in the fall when you look in the mirror and realize who you have become.

I met pure evil on this day
He seemed familiar I hate to say
I stood and wondered why that was
What's his purpose or just because
I tried to leave him, I looked away
but could not resist no how, no way
His ever present, unstabling hand
I could not flee, I could not stand
So I accepted the cold hard fact
that no one's untouched, left in-tact
for in each person both good and bad
and choices therefore must be had.

J. Darryl Harpool, with permission

Let me introduce you to some real people I've met. A few I met while I was at the bottom, some on the way up, and others as their pastor as they accepted God's mercy, which forgives, and God's grace, which restores. *The stories I use in this book are real. To modify the old television show* Dragnet's *opening: "The names (and gender, location, and stories) have been changed to protect the formerly guilty but now fully forgiven and restored."*

TIM (NOT HIS REAL NAME)

Tim called and said, "I've lost everything. Everything. I'm sleeping in my car, my wife is divorcing me, and my kids won't talk to me."

I responded, "What happened?" The last time I had talked with Tim, he was an executive with a Fortune 500 company, an elder in his church, and happily married with three beautiful kids and a house with a pool. He was well respected in the community.

Tim continued his story:

> It started two years ago when I was at a convention. I was invited up to the executive's suite of a vendor who was sponsoring the convention. When I got there, twenty to thirty of the top executives in our industry were partying. My contact to the convention sponsor told me to enjoy whatever I wanted and look around. As I entered the upstairs room, there

was cocaine spread across multiple glass tables. They offered it, and I accepted. Instantly, I felt like, "What problems?" I had been so stressed with the pressures of work, raising a family, church expectations, and paying for my kids' colleges, and with one snort, I was invincible.

I was in shock—not that Tim had made a mistake, but that I was just now hearing about it when it was too late to undo the damage. I've never known a person who, under the right circumstances, didn't make mistakes. Before you get self-righteous and tell yourself you would never fall, consider these men and women:

- ➤ King David committed adultery and murder.
- ➤ Paul was judgmental and a mass murderer of Christians.
- ➤ The Samaritan woman was cheating and on husband number five.
- ➤ Moses was a murderer and had anger issues that caused him to miss the Promised Land.
- ➤ Peter denied Jesus three times mere hours after promising complete loyalty.

Jesus's family ancestry is full of person after person with moral failures. I know they don't teach that version in most churches, but they should. I find it comforting that Jesus's own human family was as dysfunctional as the rest of us. The opening lines of Matthew, thus the first words of the New Testament, list the genealogy of Jesus. It lists forty-two ancestors from Abraham to Christ. Among them are:

> ➤ Jacob, who wrestled with God one night to such an extent he was permanently injured (scars just like us).
> ➤ Ruth, a relative of Jesus, who wasn't even an Israelite but rather a Moabite, an outcast (just like some of us). She would become the mother of Jesse, who became the father of King David (God's beloved).
> ➤ Two other women in Jesus's ancestry were Tamar, a Canaanite who committed incest (Genesis 38), and Rahab, a Jericho prostitute.

I find it reassuring that the gospel, the "good news," opens with a clear message that the promises in the Bible are for the fallen, the broken, and the ruined. In Jesus's ancestry, you have adulterers, prostitutes, disloyal friends, dysfunctional families, murderers, and outsiders. The law of the Old Testament would exclude all of them from mercy and grace. Jesus *included* people just like them. The most common question Jesus was asked was, "Why do you run with those people?" He answered, "For the Son of Man came to seek and to save the lost" (Luke 19:10).

Seeking and saving the lost … that's mercy. Just because Jesus was a perfect human and perfect God doesn't mean he didn't understand the imperfect. He spent his entire time on earth surrounded by and seeking out the ordinary and the imperfect. Jesus also said, "The thief comes only to steal and kill and destroy. I have come that they may have life, and have it to the full" (John 10:10).

I don't need to tell you about the thieves:

- Substance abuse that filled that hole in your soul for a month before the destruction starts.
- Unfaithfulness that made you feel young and wanted until it was discovered and everything important to you—family, friends and reputation—was gone.
- Being a workaholic, which initially got you promotions and income but at a price far higher than the return.
- Stealing, which at first was thrilling and rewarding because of the immediate gratification but later placed you in a cell.
- Childhood scars that you refused to deal with, which grew and manifested themselves into an adult who could no longer control the anger.
- Get-rich schemes that didn't make you rich, only ashamed.
- Selling yourself for immediate gratification that left you feeling dirty.
- Pornography that was immediately exciting but eventually took control of your soul and set unrealistic expectations.
- Abandonment that initially made it seem like the easy life but couldn't ease your mind.
- Dreams that were yours but not God's and now lay scattered on the floor.
- Incest that you blame yourself for despite being the victim and now anger consumes you.

Thieves come to prevent you from being what God had planned for you. Being outside the will of God is horrible. If you were once close to God and then fell, being outside of the will of God is miserable. Jesus came to forgive and restore those whose lives are broken, crippled, and ruined. To forgive and restore the outcast. To forgive and restore those from even the most hideous dysfunctional family. He still has a plan for you, and it is a good one.

We fall because we are human, and all of us have fallen short. Tim got addicted to cocaine and added alcohol (which he had problems with in his youth). He wiped out the checking account, savings account, retirement fund, kid's college fund, and eventually the corporate credit card. The Fortune 500 Company fired him. His church judged and condemned him. Jesus is mercy and grace, but some churches kill their wounded. I know it is not what churches are supposed to do, but many of them give less mercy and grace than the local country club and not near as much as the local pub.

Tim eventually lost everything and had been living in his car for about two years when he borrowed a cell phone and called me. I want to write, "And then he recommitted his life to Jesus and turned it all around." However, the truth is there would be many more falls. He was in and out of treatment, lying and stealing from family and friends, and there was still no reconciliation with his wife or kids. There would be missed birthdays, graduations, weddings, and birth of grandkids. Tim is making it back slowly and painfully and with hard work. Jesus, through his mercy, forgave Tim for his sins. God is restoring Tim through grace, but sin will take you further than you want to go.

LAURIE (NOT HER REAL NAME)

Laurie was the beautiful daughter of the senior pastor of an exceptional church in the West. I was speaking there one Sunday, but before I spoke, she gave her testimony. Laurie was a recent graduate in political science from a prestigious university. She was climbing fast when she met a married legislator. She was attracted to him in every way. The legislator was in the second decade of marriage when the burdens of raising children, paying bills, saving for college, working lots of hours, and losing hair and fitness sometimes occur. Quite frankly, Laurie was the best-looking woman to show interest in him in years. Laurie made no demands on the legislator: no help with the diapers, attending school meetings, spending time at home, or other normal, but sometimes mind-numbing, aspects of our lives.

The legislator woke up and realized that he loved his kids, if not his wife, more than he loved feeling younger and being admired again. He dumped Laurie. Laurie filled the hole left by the affair with alcohol and meaningless sex, and eventually sought counseling. However, the problem with falls is that the damage to our "right and wrong" compass recovers slowly. She ended up in an affair with the associate pastor at the church her father led, and eventually the scandal caused the church to lose two pastors and a family to move away and start all over.

Tim and Laurie's stories may seem extreme, but just off the top of my head, I could provide real stories about:

➢ A young high school teacher who, although she was just four years older than the senior boy, didn't realize the consequences of the relationship. The boy moved away, and she lives on the other side of the country, trying to recover from being labeled a sex offender.

➢ A star athlete and student-body president who sent inappropriate texts that were shared and became a front-page story. This resulted in him being a registered predator.

➢ A successful businessman who lied early in his marriage and then got the call nineteen years later that he had another daughter. He had to tell his wife and kids there were other kids.

➢ A pastor who had to tell his congregation he had stolen $30,000 from the church after fourteen years of faithful service.

➢ A banker who was caught with sickening child pornography by his fourteen-year-old daughter, who thought he was a role model.

➢ A mother who was convicted of vehicular manslaughter and had to say goodbye to her four- and six-year-old children for the next ten years.

➢ A builder who gave his family a better life than he could afford by cheating on his taxes, which wiped out his family for restoration. He has two years to serve in federal prison, and his reputation is destroyed.

➢ A police officer who began to keep part of the illegal narcotics he confiscated and later was arrested for breaking into the home of his neighbor of twenty-five years and stealing pain killers.

➢ A public official arrested for shoplifting wine so no one would know he drank.

➢ A lawyer who swindled clients and then, when caught, shot herself in the head, leaving her family in ruin.

➢ A college president who sought compensation and recognition to the point his career came crashing down as the college financially collapsed.

➢ A former college professor who passed out behind a bar in -10 degree weather and froze to death.

➢ An elder in the church who was so abusive to his son that his son, at nineteen years old, murdered two people for $70.

It took no notes and about ten minutes for me to come up with that list. I could fill pages with similar falls, and a couple of them would be my own stories. We all have stories, or as a church I once attended said, "Me too."

I was in a church service one Sunday when the ushers passed out a piece of paper. On it were statements such as:

_____I have abused another human being.

_____I have abused alcohol.

_____I have used another person knowing I was using them.

_____I judge people based on their appearance.

_____I've stolen money or property that wasn't mine.

19

_____I've lied to cover up my own mistakes.

_____I've cheated on my taxes.

_____I routinely take drugs to escape reality.

_____I've committed adultery.

You get the idea. There were other questions but with the same focus. They had every person in attendance complete the survey but made it clear to leave our names off of it. They had us pass them down the row, face down. They collected the surveys, and we went on with the worship service. About ten minutes later, the ushers reappeared. They started handing out the completed surveys collected earlier to the opposite side of the large five-thousand-person auditorium. We each got a completed survey, but it wasn't ours; it was someone present in the service, but a stranger, or at least someone unidentified. Then the pastor asked us to please stand if there was a *yes* marked on the survey as he read each question. Tears ran down my face as I realized we were all fallen people.

You might be thinking that we're not all fallen people, but that tells me you haven't had the fall. And I hope you don't. There are millions of people out there who have had the fall. We made horrible decisions with equally horrible consequences and just can't figure out how to get back up. Haven't you ever wondered …?

- Where did the Reason family go? They don't attend anymore.
- Where is Bob? I haven't seen him since the divorce.

- What happened to that young, dynamic preacher? He just disappeared.
- Why did Mr. Elk leave teaching? He was a tremendous science teacher.
- Whatever happened to the attorney, Mr. Welk, who got the DWI? Did he move?
- Why does Kelly hop from one bad relationship to another?
- Why doesn't Steve seek public office? He'd be a great leader.

THE NONSENSE OF "WHEN YOU GET RIGHT, COME BACK"

The reason many who have taken the fall don't think mercy that forgives and grace that restores is available to them, is because they have been told a lie. You remember that earlier we discussed the lie that someone can "fall from grace." The second lie, equally unsupported in the Bible, is, "When you get right, come back to church." They've been told they are not welcome. Oh, not necessarily with those words, but with the attitude that the church is for perfect people. Pardon me for being blunt. Actually, don't. That attitude is not from Jesus; it is the opposite of Jesus. It reminds me of a woman who told a pastor mentor of mine, "I'm leaving this church to find one without so many problems." My mentor responded, "If you find the perfect church, please don't join it; you will ruin it."

If you treat fallen people with that attitude of "get it all together and then come back," you are a contributor to the very reason they will never experience restoring grace. People don't get right and then go to church. They come to church and experience Jesus, and then they get right.

In the Bible, there is a story of a woman (John, Chapter 8) that the self-righteous grace-deniers were getting ready to stone. Jesus, of course, stopped them by shaming them by telling the one without sin to cast the first stone. Telling someone to get right before they come to your church, is like saying to the cheating woman about to be stoned, that she should get right, just after they stone her to death.

Ask any kid whose family was dysfunctional what it is like to watch families who appear perfect at school, community, and church events. It reinforces what they already believe: "There is something wrong with me." They're right in the sense that there is something wrong with all of us. The lie is that your sins are worse than other people's. We are fallen people in a fallen world. I encourage our members to leave the masks at home and dress up for Halloween. We are all, at one time or another, broken people.

But we don't have to live like fallen people in a fallen world. God loves us too much to leave us as we are. Your past has nothing to do with your future in Jesus. Easter wasn't for the perfect people or perfect families or perfect churches, because they don't exist. It is all a façade. They are just good at wearing masks. Masks are accepted and even encouraged by some churches. Easter is for the fallen, who need forgiveness and grace that restores, which only a savior can provide. Jesus offers mercy that forgives and grace that restores to:

> ➤ the tax collector who stole from everyone
> ➤ the Roman guard who ignored faith, too busy until his daughter was sick
> ➤ the prostitute
> ➤ the crippled—some physically and all emotionally
> ➤ the lame, in the many forms of lameness
> ➤ the mentally and physically abused
> ➤ the weak
> ➤ the outcast
> ➤ the poor
> ➤ the powerless
> ➤ the blind: physically, racially, and otherwise
> ➤ the rich guy who can't figure out what's missing
> ➤ the lovers who never get loved in return
> ➤ the faithful who are treated with disloyalty
> ➤ the faithless who doesn't know whether or not there is a God
> ➤ the confused for whom life doesn't make sense
> ➤ the dreamer whose dreams are scattered on the floor

Easter says your worst day, year, decade, or even entire life up until now doesn't have to define you; Jesus will. The canvas of your life can be painted again. As comedian and singer Mark Lowry says, "Aren't you glad your worst day doesn't define you?" I am.

You may be thinking, *you don't know what I've done.* No, I don't, but Jesus does. And he knows the things you thought about doing but didn't and the really awful things you thought about doing and did. And yet while we were sinners, he loved us so much, he died for us (Romans 5:8).

He didn't just love sinners, he forgave them (mercy) and restored them (grace). Jesus restored them and then put them to work for his kingdom. Jesus used adulterers, murderers, thieves, oppressors, the oppressed, and every one in-between, because your past has nothing to do with your future in Jesus.

Remember those awful commercials of an elderly person lying on the floor, talking to the camera while pushing a button for help: "Help, I've fallen, and I can't get up." That is right. On our own power we cannot get back up. Let Jesus pick you up. My guess is that one of three things is true if you're not back where you should be in God's plan.

1. You don't really believe you're forgiven (mercy forgives).
2. You don't really believe that grace can restore you to where God intended you to be (grace restores).
3. You believe in mercy and grace intellectually, but you haven't started claiming your rights as a child of God, to be forgiven and loved.

I encourage you to continue with me in this book. I remember the hopelessness of *falleness*. Falleness means the quality of being fallen or degraded. I remember that feeling and wondering how I got there. I'd ask that question for another five years.

CHAPTER 3

How Falls Happen

M ax Lucado, in his book *God is With You Every Day,* writes:

> David dedicated a season of his life to making stupid, idiotic, godless decisions. Yes, David! King David! The man after God's own heart suppressed his wrongdoing and paid a steep price for doing so. He later described it this way: "When I refused to confess my sin, my body wasted away, and I groaned all day long … my strength evaporated like water in the summer heat" (Psalm 32:3–4 NLT). Sin's reality replaced sin's euphoria. He finally prayed, "LORD, do not forsake me; do not be far from me, my God. Come quickly to help me, my Lord and my Savior" (Psalm 38:21–22 NIV). Bury misbehavior and expect pain—period! You cannot escape the misery is creates, unless you

pray as David did: "Come quickly to help me,
my Lord and my Savior." Then, grace will come.

Falling is a process. My fall, and maybe yours, went like this:

Fall One: I made some dumb decisions, at least dumb in terms
of timing and situation.

Fall Two: I felt rejected by church and community folks as the
rumor mill piled on (the wildest one was that I killed a custodian;
I have no idea where in the world that came from). I understand
the role of accountability in the church and especially for
committed Christians, but starting with accountability, for
someone who just fell, is like a parent punishing a child who
didn't know what they did was wrong, while telling them the
punishment is a reward.

Fall Three: I felt all alone, and instead of finding good, God-
seeking people who understood mercy that forgives and grace
that restores, I sought out instant acceptance. I sought out
people who wouldn't immediately judge me. Other fallen people,
whether at the gym, the bar, school, or work, are accepting.
When you're fallen, you don't have time to judge; you are just
happy people are around you and not bringing up the fall.

Fall Four: You make it worse by doubling down to mask the
guilt and hurt, or you move away from all your support with
the idea of starting over. Sometimes starting over is the right
move, but not until you've accepted God's mercy and grace and

really believe it applies to you. Not until you've started living like you're forgiven. You may not recognize it, but down deep, you say to yourself, "Well if that's who they think I am, that's who I'll be." I remember thinking, *If they think I'm wild, I'll show them wild.* Of course that is stupid thinking, but we don't make our best decisions when we're on the bottom and our backs are against the wall.

Fall Five: Find your bottom, rock bottom, and then go a little lower, and then lower. Okay, now you've hit bottom. At this point there are two choices: stay there, which many of us do, or get up. The same power that resurrected Jesus will do the same for your life, now and in eternity.

I was sitting across from a guy in a sandwich shop, and he saw my Bible. He said, "You go to church?"

I said, "Yes, I'm a believer."

He said, "I used to be active in a small church, never missed a service."

I asked, "Why did you stop?"

He said, "Prison, divorce, drug abuse, alcohol, couldn't keep a job."

I said, "Okay, made some mistakes. Haven't we all."

He responded, "You don't know what I've done. Too hard to get back. As my ex-wife said, 'Too much water under the bridge.'"

I said, "You ask for God's forgiveness?" He said he did. I asked, "Did you ask for God's grace?" He said yes. So I asked,

"Then why aren't you active in a church now and living for Jesus?"

He said, "I'm just not comfortable at church, and when people find out about me, they don't want anything to do with me. All church does is make me feel worse."

I relate to Steve ... that longing to restore what I had lost, especially the fellowship with Jesus and a church that treats you like family. Missing what you had or always wanted can cause an ache in your soul. I've been in churches like that. Again, let me be blunt: the world doesn't need another voice, especially a church, telling people they are bad and rotten and a disappointment to God and their families. I understand the need to talk of sin to those who don't understand their need for Jesus. But a church that every Sunday, just reminds people how awful they are and doesn't discuss mercy that forgives and grace that restores, is like a prison that doesn't attempt rehabilitation; its goal is punishment and condemnation.

Terry grew up in a church like that: nothing but judgment and condemnation. His mother made him go every time the door opened. Terry married a committed Christian, but he made going to church so miserable for her (even though they went to a positive, mercy- and grace-filled church) that she quit. She made sure the kids went, but she missed out on worship for over fifty years. Terry was a good man, just completely turned off by church. The result was when Terry died, his wife went back to the church for the last ten years of her life, and while blessed by the reconnection, she also had fifty years of regret. It started with a church that preached condemnation despite the

Bible stating unequivocally, "There is now no condemnation for those who are in Christ Jesus" (Romans 8:1).

I think some of the churches are just misguided. Others intentionally know they can manipulate giving and attendance through guilt. Jesus never *guilted* someone into submission. Guilted is when you make someone feel guilty or take advantage of the fact they already feel guilty, to induce them into doing something you want them to do. Unfortunately, sometimes that is some churches. Jesus didn't use guilt to manipulate others, rather he loved people into becoming who God created them to be.

I might have never taken a step up from the bottom. From the world's perspective, I was good at bottom living. I made a good living, was the life of any party, and tried to treat others fairly. I was a good friend to other friends. So, what's the problem with bottom living? The problem is that bottom living is not living the life God intended, for the purpose intended, to accomplish the outcomes he intended for the kingdom of God. Living outside of God's will is unfulfilling. Living outside of God's will while knowing God's will for your life is a horrible existence. You can be a prodigal son and yet still be living in the penthouse.

I might still be on the bottom except for a local pastor whom I knew of, but who barely knew me. Ron called and said, "Let's have lunch. God wants us to." I met Ron, and we talked. I started down the road of all my mistakes and what I had lost and things I'd never accomplish for God because of my past mistakes. He said, "David, you have two problems. One,

29

you think your mistakes [the way we discuss sin, but he used another term] are worse [actually smell worse] than everybody else's. Second, I should have brought you a white robe. If you are going to play God in your life, you should dress the part." I laughed, but I got his point.

I look back now and think, *How arrogant of me.* I had decided the weight of my sin. I had decided the limits on God's grace. I had concluded what God would or wouldn't do. I had God in a box as small as I felt. Ron went on to say, "I hear you've led music and youth at some churches, and God blessed it. Come do that with me." I did for a few years as I healed and learned to depend on God again. I learned to trust him even when I didn't trust myself.

There are two important concepts here: First, God doesn't reluctantly or begrudgingly give us mercy (forgiveness) and grace (restoration). Ephesians 1:7–8 tells us, "In Him we have redemption through his blood, the forgiveness of sins, [mercy that forgives] in accordance with the riches of God's grace [that restores] that he lavished on us."

Lavish means "to bestow (give) something in generous or extravagant quantities." Some people and churches are stingy with forgiveness and grace. God is not stingy with his forgiveness and grace. God paid for forgiveness with the blood of Jesus and he lavishes his grace on us- grace that can restore.

There were other falls, bumps, and bruises, which I'll share as we work our way to mercy that forgives and grace that restores. But believe me, God has a plan to stop falls from becoming fatal. There are God-given steps to prevent fatal falls.

If you're one of those folks who hasn't made mistakes and has no scars or blemishes—pretty much always lived for Jesus without a misstep or fall—you can quit reading. The story of mercy that forgives and grace that restores, while learning to live like someone forgiven, is for the rest of us.

CHAPTER 4

EXACTLY WHAT WE DIDN'T NEED

It is not by accident that when we fall, we run into exactly the type of people we do not need. That's not an accident or coincidence that happens; it's because of intentional evil. If Satan can keep you down and out, he can keep you from accomplishing what God created you to do. I know if you are at the bottom, thinking there is something you can do for God is the furthest thing from your mind. The good and truthful news is that God is not finished with you. God has not abandoned you. God still has a plan for your life. But be aware, evil will do everything it can to keep you down.

GRACE-DENIERS

I understand every one of the conditions we want to place on getting well and being whole. I know how a lot of conditions developed. Somewhere along your fall, during the mistake(s), you experienced the self-righteous grace-deniers that pushed you back down or contributed to a second or third or fourth fall. Self-righteous grace-deniers are not about the love of Jesus, which is shown through his mercy (forgiveness) and grace (restoration). Self-righteous grace-deniers are about making themselves feel better by piling on you, on your way to the bottom. They use the term "fall from grace." They are the type of people who kick you when you're down. You know the ones who mask what they're doing with phrases such as, "God bless poor Rob; you know he has a real drinking problem." The purpose of their statement wasn't really to ask God to bless Rob; it was to make sure everyone knows Rob is a drunk. Self-righteous grace-deniers intentionally ignore the fact that "all have sin and fall short" (Romans 3:23).

Grace-deniers have created a hierarchy of sin. Grace-deniers have much more in common with the Pharisees of Jesus's time than Jesus. Jesus made it clear how he viewed self-righteous grace-deniers in Matthew 23:13–33, where he reprimanded them seven times and concluded with verse 33, "You snakes! You brood of vipers! How will you escape being condemned to Hell?"

A hierarchy of sin is when we say some sins are worse than other sins. We then decide the sins of our neighbors, brothers, sisters, parents, spouses, or church staff are bad sins and our sins aren't that big of deal. That type of thinking is delusional. (My guess is most of you reading this have the opposite problem in that you believe your sins are worse than others.) It is especially bad when you're hitting bottom and you meet one of these grace-deniers. I bet you have experienced one of these grace-deniers. The grace-deniers haven't accepted restoring grace for themselves, so it is impossible for them to give it away. They can't risk loving others because they don't know what it is like to be loved. Philip Yancey, in his book *What's So Amazing about Grace?* observed:

> One who has been touched by grace will no longer look on those who stray as "those evil people" or "those poor people who need our help." Nor must we search for signs of "love worthiness." Grace teaches us that God loves because of who God is, not because of who we are.

There is a reason why the Bible says, "By this [love] everyone will know that you are my [Jesus's] disciples" (John 13:35). Notice, it doesn't say that by *doctrine perfection,* everyone will know you are a Christian. I am not suggesting that it doesn't make any difference how the scripture is interpreted. Rather, I'm arguing love and acceptance come first. I am echoing the old song, "if you believe in Jesus, you belong with me".

I remember a time when I had two chances, early after my fall, to get back up and stay on the plan God had for me. Both times, the same grace-denier made calls to ensure that the two organizations wouldn't take a chance on me. She didn't do it out of genuine concern but rather because it made her feel better. It was an interesting night a few years later when I saw her and the husband of another member of the church going into a seedy hotel at the other end of town. I just prayed for her, and that was freeing.

Chuck Swindoll tells the story of the late Welsh minister Martyn Lloyd-Jones, who once said:

> Preaching grace is not only risky, but the fact that some take it to unwise extremes proves that we are preaching the true grace of God. Some will take advantage of such teaching. They will misrepresent it. They will go so far as to promote the wrong idea that you can go on sinning as much as you like. The idea of grace has always been controversial. It brings grace-abusers as well as grace-killers out from under the rocks! Paul met them head-on in the first century; we must do the same in the twenty-first.

Pockets Full of Rocks

Grace-deniers are like the crowd in the following story, who were ready to stone to death a woman they didn't know but were willing to judge.

> John 8:4 {the Pharisees} said to Jesus, "Teacher, this woman was caught in the act of adultery. 5 In the Law Moses commanded us to stone such women. Now what do you say?" 6 They were using this question as a trap, in order to have a basis for accusing him. But Jesus bent

down and started to write on the ground with his finger. 7 When they kept on questioning him, he straightened up and said to them, "Let any one of you who is without sin be the first to throw a stone at her." 8 Again he stooped down and wrote on the ground. 9 At this, those who heard began to go away one at a time, the older ones first, until only Jesus was left, with the woman still standing there. 10 Jesus straightened up and asked her, "Woman, where are they? Has no one condemned you?" 11 "No one, sir," she said. "Then neither do I condemn you," Jesus declared. "Go now and leave your life of sin."

Grace-deniers carry pockets full of rocks, ready to judge and condemn at any opportunity. Notice Jesus's instruction, "Go now and leave your life of sin." Jesus didn't say, "Go and carry guilt forever." Jesus didn't say, "Go and you are sort of restored." Most important, Jesus didn't say, "Go, get yourself right, clean up, dress up, attend church, and then I'll restore you." Jesus said, "Then neither do I condemn you." If Jesus doesn't condemn you, why would you let the grace-deniers?

THE PRODIGAL'S BROTHER SYNDROME

The story of the prodigal son is a powerful story in the Bible. It can be used to teach a bad gospel that focuses only on the sinfulness of the prodigal son. Most of the time, it is used appropriately to describe the over-the-top love of the father no matter what we've done. Rarer, but equally important, it can be used to teach how we all need mercy and grace.

When the prodigal returned home and the father threw the party and restored his son to his proper role, the brother of the prodigal son struggled with the celebration. It didn't seem fair that he had stayed and done what his father asked while the prodigal brother was out wasting money and embarrassing his family. The Prodigal's Brother Syndrome is when we are so focused on the mistakes of others and our human sense of fairness that we miss our own faults and mistakes. The syndrome is when, rather than celebrating the return and restoration of a brother, we focus on the magnitude of the prodigal's fall and our sense of self-righteousness. If you have taken a fall, you have dealt with grace-deniers and those who have the Prodigal's Brother Syndrome.

TOO MUCH GRACE—PURE ABSURDITY

You have also probably experienced people who have said we shouldn't get carried away by grace. Their argument is that if we talk too much about grace, people will keep on doing what they want without reference to God's calling or purpose in our lives. They argue, "People will sin because they can."

I don't think that's true. Most people who have been right with God desperately want to be right with God again, but due to a fall, they don't know how. It's a rare person who genuinely experiences mercy that forgives and grace that restores and sees it as a license to sin as much as possible. More likely, they sin because they have fallen short and gotten into a never-ending cycle of bottom-feeding, which we will discuss next.

Churches and others, limit grace because it's easier to understand if there are conditions and limits. Grace with limits makes sense. Grace without limits is so God-like. Limited grace fits in my box, my small version of God. Unlimited grace is scandalous. It's outside my wiring. Churches can get conformity and order by emphasizing rule- and law-based grace. Churches only change communities when they share unlimited, amazing grace.

So, before you say, "I've tried grace, and it didn't work," let's explore, later in the book, not just saving grace, but restoring grace—unlimited, scandalous grace.

BOTTOM-FEEDERS

You've probably heard of fish that are bottom-feeders. One of the characteristics of bottom-feeders is that most can bury themselves. They bury themselves so as not to be seen until they pounce on food. They exist to devour whatever they see.

My guess is you've met a bottom-feeder—someone so far away from God's purpose for them that they've hit bottom, stayed there, and now devour other human beings who've stumbled. They accept everyone, pass no judgment, and draw you in close. Then they pounce. Sometimes they're codependents, pimps, drug dealers, or human traffickers. Other times they will simply claim to be your friend or lover. Bottom-feeders are every bit as dangerous to getting back up, as self-righteous grace-deniers. Their interest is only in picking at the bones of what is left of the person God created you to be. A former mentor of mine used to hold up a rose at all baby dedications. He would then remind the parents and others in attendance, that if we let the world, it will pick every flower off the rose, until there is only a stem. Bottom-feeders will wait until a person is down and then pick them clean of any remaining self-esteem leaving only the shell of the person create by God.

Bottom-feeders will sell us on the idea that we're rescuing them, which appeals to us, because even when we're fallen, we have a need to occasionally do something good. Temporarily doing something good clears our conscience, but it doesn't last. We can't earn or work our way to God's approval. We can only accept what he's already done for us on the cross—while we were sinners. If you try to rescue bottom-feeders before you are fully restored through Jesus, you will be sucked into destructive relationships and behaviors. The bottom-feeder will feed on you and you on them, in mutual destruction. Bottom-feeders are hoping you will stay down and never get up. Misery loves company.

PAT

Pat was a good preacher. The problem was, Pat's wife wanted nothing to do with the ministry anymore. In her defense, the church Pat pastored thought they had hired Pat as pastor and his wife as the church servant. Finally, she had enough, and when Pat wouldn't stand up to the bullies at the church, she confused her frustration with no longer loving Pat. She divorced Pat, the church fired him (again killing the wounded), and Pat began to find more "grace" in the local pub. Every time Pat got close to serving another church, someone would block him, not understanding the circumstances, or at least not caring. Last time I saw him, he was drunk, bitter, and angry with God. God gets a lot of blame for things some of his followers do. I saw a bumper sticker recently that said, "God, protect me from your followers."

God can and will protect you from self-righteous grace-deniers, from those living the Prodigal's Brother Syndrome, from those who hold back on grace so there isn't too much, and from bottom-feeders.

Enough about grace-deniers, the Prodigal's Brother Syndrome, the too-much-grace mentality, and bottom-feeders. It is time for you and me to stop using them as an excuse for why we're not getting off the bottom; accepting God's mercy, which forgives all sin; and God's restoring grace, which will put you on the path to being exactly what God created you to be. As the Reverend Billy Sunday said about hypocrites, "I'd rather go to church with a few of them then to hell with the rest." The following poem walks us through despair to the ever-slight flicker of hope. In Jesus, it is never over, never too late, never final.

Life imagined, life dismissed
Life forgotten, life remiss
Life subjected to every pain
Suffer loss - forget the gain
Pain imagined, pain dismissed
Pain forgotten, pain remiss
Pain neglected, pain forgot
Ever suffer, feel the loss
Grace imagined, grace dismissed
Grace forgotten, grace remiss
Grace neglected, grace forgot
Ever searching, for your lot
Love imagined, love dismissed
Love forgotten, love remiss
Love subjected to every pain
Hopeless, daunted full of shame
Hope imagined, hope dismissed
Hope forgotten, hope remiss
Hope eternal, hope surrounds
Endless, flawless with no bounds.
J. Darryl Harpool with Permission

CHAPTER 5

STOPPING THE STORM CYCLE, FINDING SHELTER

I f you have fallen, then you know the feeling of being sick and tired of being sick and tired. When you've hit bottom, it is very difficult not to keep repeating bad choices and making bad decisions. When you are in a bad place, it is easy for bad things to find and follow you. The conscience isn't a good sleep aid.

There is a reason addictions often travel in pairs. While you are in the shame stage, making bad decisions is easier than making the changes needed. Yet, it is imperative that when you hit bottom, you find a shelter where you can think clearly and see objectively. Clear vision and rational thoughts usually don't come while you're falling. You need a shelter from your storm—somewhere you can quit focusing on the storm and damage done and start focusing on the necessary changes. In Luke 8:22–39, we find the disciples, those closest to Jesus, in a physical storm and, for some of them, a personal storm.

> One day Jesus said to his disciples, "Let us go
> over to the other side of the lake." So they got
> into a boat and set out. As they sailed, he fell
> asleep. A squall came down on the lake, so that
> the boat was being swamped, and they were in
> great danger. (v. 22–23)

You might be thinking, *I don't need a Bible story right now.*
Yes, you do; you really need this story. Note the disciples were
on a journey, and the storm hit. We don't wake up one day and
say, "Let's go make a mess of our lives. Let's destroy all our
relationships, damage our futures, and lose everything." No,
most of our falls come in the middle of doing what we did every
day, trying to make a living and live our lives. The disciples had
been in that boat on that lake and had crossed it many times.
This time was different. This time there was an unexpected
storm.

IT DOESN'T MATTER WHO CAUSED THE STORM—NOT WHILE YOU ARE IN IT

The same is likely true for you. A little mistake led to more
mistakes, which led to a big mistake and then to a lifestyle
of mistakes, to the point where all you could see, everywhere
you looked, was the storm and the storm damage. It doesn't
matter whether or not you caused the storm, encouraged the
storm, or found yourself the victim of the storm; it was still a
storm. Storms destroy and kill, regardless of their cause. Your

role in causing the storm may be important later as you get off the bottom but not while you are in the midst of it and getting battered on every side.

The Worst Thing You Can Do

The disciples did the worst thing you can do when you are in a storm: they panicked. When you and I panic, it makes a few things happen, and none of them are good. First, when we panic, we turn the focus on us and the impact of the storm, instead of getting out of the storm. Second, when we panic, we focus on the storm's power and not on God's power. Third, when we panic, we limit our ability to think and to control our emotions. The disciples panicked. "The disciples went and woke him, saying, 'Master, Master, we're going to drown!'" (v. 24). I am not saying there isn't real damage possible in a storm. Storms are real, and as some of us know, storms can alter the rest of our lives. The disciples were not wrong for identifying the storm; they were correct. "A squall came down on the lake, so that the boat was being swamped, and they were in great danger" (v. 23). Their mistake was focusing on the storm and not on God. When we hit bottom, the most important thing we can do is to focus on what God told us.

- I won't abandon you. (Hebrews 13:5–6)
- Cast your cares on me for I care for you. (1 Peter 5:7)
- Fear not. (2 Timothy 1:7)
- I will always forgive you. (1 John 1:9)

OUR CIRCUMSTANCES DO NOT DEFINE US. GOD DOES.

The disciples made the classic bad decision that can be made during storms. They evaluated their circumstances instead of their God. Their circumstances were that they had a lot of people in a small boat, on waves, in the midst of water, with a high probability of drowning. While that is an accurate description of their circumstances, it is not an accurate description of their situation. God hadn't spoken yet to their situation. Come to think of it, where was God? "As they sailed, he fell asleep" (v. 23).

Don't miss this. It wasn't that the disciples couldn't feel God in their situation or that they didn't know where he was or how any of this mess could be used by God to fulfill his plan for them. Jesus was literally asleep. It's okay; admit it. When you're hitting bottom, it's easy to feel that God is asleep on the job.

- Diagnosis of cancer? He's sleeping.
- Child out of control? He's sleeping.
- Abusive spouse? He's sleeping.
- Loss of a loved one? He's sleeping.
- Broken marriage? He's sleeping.
- Ministry destroyed? He's sleeping.
- Reputation ruined? He's sleeping.
- Developing an addiction? He's sleeping.

Don't confuse your unhappiness or a lack of understanding of your current circumstances with God not caring. Your circumstances do not determine how much God loves you;

rather your circumstances measure how much grace he will give you. His grace is sufficient. Faith is when you know God loves you, he is in charge, and he has a plan for you even when your circumstances suggest he's asleep.

YOUR PAST HAS NOTHING TO DO WITH YOUR FUTURE IN JESUS

The truth is that sometimes it does seem like God is asleep. In the case of the disciples in the boat, being swamped by waves, he was … but he was also still in control. One reason Jesus was asleep was simply, he was tired. However, another reason why Jesus was asleep is that he was at peace with the storm. He knew the storm could mold the disciples into whom they were created to be. He knew he would protect them, so he was at peace. If we could remember and honestly believe one thing in the storms of life, we would avoid our falls. That one truth is:

God has a plan for your life. You and I can't prevent God from being God simply because we are being human. His plan for us is based on his love for us, and he will work his plan for us and for our good, if we submit to him. That is true no matter how far off the path we've gone. Your past has nothing to do with your future in Jesus. Your circumstances don't define you, God does.

Saul was a killer of Christians before he was Paul. I'm pretty sure you're not further away from God's plan for your life than that: admit it. I meet people who have taken a fall and they, like me, focus on how bad they have been, how awful they are, and the magnitude of their sins. That's ego and Satan. To be blunt, no matter how much you've messed up your life, you're a rookie compared to Paul (Saul), the mass murderer of the followers of Jesus. Yet, when Paul turned to Jesus, God put him on the path he intended for Paul, and it changed his world.

WHERE TO FIND REST IN THE MIDST OF THE STORM?

The greatest storm shelter of all time is Jesus. "He got up and rebuked the wind and the raging waters; the storm subsided, and all was calm" (v. 24). Jesus spoke peace to their circumstances, but more important he demonstrated control over their situation. He did all this while still waking up. He raised Lazarus from the dead, after being four days late. Your life may be a mess, but you're still breathing—maybe barely, but you haven't been rotting in the ground for four days. Even death isn't impossible for Jesus to overcome; think what he can and will do for your mess.

THE CATCH

However, to find peace in the midst of the storm, to prevent from drowning as you hit bottom, there is something you need to do. Jesus asked a simple question: "'Where is your faith?' he asked his disciples. In fear and amazement they asked one another, 'Who is this? He commands even the winds and the water, and they obey him'" (v. 25).

Notice the disciples were still in fear, but it was turning to amazement as they watched Jesus, straight from a nap, speak peace to their circumstance. He controlled their situation. Then they remembered, this is Jesus. They put their faith in him. They didn't completely understand who Jesus was yet, and neither do we, but they put their faith in him that even the winds and water obey.

WILL YOU?

Nothing I've written in this book will help you if you don't take that first step and place your faith in Jesus. He is trustworthy. Just ask:

- ➤ The woman at the well with a history of broken relationships
- ➤ Lazarus, dead for four days
- ➤ The man, chained in a cave, who had more demons than the town had people
- ➤ The soldier whose servant was healed without Jesus even showing up in person
- ➤ The father of the daughter who Jesus healed from certain death
- ➤ The man who was crippled and lived on a mat for thirty-eight years, until Jesus said, "Get up."
- ➤ The woman who was healed just by touching the garment of Jesus

> ➢ Hundreds of outcasts at the time of Jesus and millions since who've found out their self-worth after meeting the master
> ➢ Paul (Saul) the serial killer, just to name a few.

They all prayed, in different words with similar meaning, this:

> Jesus, my life is a mess. I am scared. My circumstances suggest that it is all over, and I am losing my life, that which I haven't already wasted. I believe you are who you say you are, the Son of God, the Messiah. I ask you to forgive me of my sins. I ask you to pick up the shattered pieces of my life and do with it whatever you want.

That prayer is how prostitutes, thieves, murderers, the self-righteous, and you and I begin to find peace in the midst of the storm.

CHAPTER 6

FORGIVENESS (MERCY), THE FIRST STEP ON THE PATH TO STANDING UP

Mercy, simply stated, is God not giving us what we deserve. Justice is a good thing when it comes to law. However, none of us should seek justice when it comes to our relationship with God. If God gave us what we deserved, none of us would like the outcome. Rather, God, through Jesus, decided to give us mercy. Mercy applied is forgiveness. Most people who have fallen know, at least theoretically, that they can ask for forgiveness and get it from a God who came to seek and save us. The problem is that theoretical forgiveness does not inspire us to get up or to try again. Theoretical forgiveness is when we limit God's forgiveness by thinking things such as:

- God forgives, but he doesn't forget.
- Even if God forgets, other people won't.

- God's forgiveness is temporary, and the next time I mess up, he'll remind me.
- God may forgive and forget, but I can't forgive myself.
- God may forgive me, and I may forgive me, but I can't forget.
- If God really forgives me, why am I suffering all these consequences of a forgiven sin?

Let's deal with each one of these individually because they're each an important lie to debunk. At one time or another, I have thought all of these. These falsehoods are pure evil, designed to convince you that your circumstances define you, when in fact, God can overcome your circumstances to restore you to what he intended you to be.

1. God forgives, but he doesn't forget.

That may be true of earthly parents concerning their daughter's boyfriend, but not our heavenly Father. In fact, God promises to:

a. Cast our sins as far as the east is from the west.
b. Cast our sins into the depths of the sea to be remembered no more.
c. Clear our record and forgive us of all transgressions

Isaiah 43:25 says, "I, even I, am he who blots out your transgressions, for my own sake, and remembers your sins no more."

There is a great gospel song by the Crabb Family that says, "I could tell you had forgotten what I was talking about." The song describes someone confessing his sin to God, knowing they had already asked and received forgiveness, and somewhere in the discussion, he can tell God has completely forgotten the subject because God forgives and forgets. When it comes to confessed sin, God has an "I don't remember" response.

2. Even if God forgets, other people won't.

To some extent, that is a true statement. The good news is that once we have accepted mercy that forgives and grace that restores, it doesn't matter. The crowd was about to stone a woman to death. Jesus wrote in the sand, "Let he who is without sin throw the first stone." The crowd dropped their stones and walked away, some in shame of self-righteousness and judgment. My guess is the woman couldn't care less what others said about her because she knew what Jesus said. To really experience the mercy of forgiveness, we have to be so thankful that we are forgiven and on the path to being restored that we don't care what a few miserable self-righteous grace-deniers think or say. We should care what Jesus says about us. The Bible tells us that Jesus is our advocate. Remember, Jesus was talked about all the time. The most common question asked of Jesus was essentially, "Why do you run around with those types?" Jesus was 100 percent human and 100 percent God. He wasn't humanlike; he was a human. He relates to you and

I because he's been there, done that. God so loved us that he let himself become human so he would be able to say, "I walked in your shoes."

When I took a fall, there was this one guy who brought up my fall every time he saw me. He used my pain and mistakes to feel better about his own poor self-esteem. The Christian approach would have been to pray for him and ignore him, if I could. Instead, I punched him. I'm not proud of it. He's the only person I have ever intentionally thrown a punch at, to hurt him. I learned quickly that accepting Jesus's view of me rather than their uniformed, self-motivated opinion was a better choice.

Most people actually forget too. The majority of people, when I opened up to them, were kind and supportive. One said to me, when I was remembering my sin, "Knock off that nonsense; you taught me that even in my imperfection, I am perfect in Jesus." I had taught that concept to many people but had to learn that it applied to me even on my worst day. Sometimes it is easier to give mercy and grace than to receive it. I am so glad my worst day doesn't define me.

3. *God's forgiveness is temporary, and the next time I mess up, he'll remind me.*

That is true of unforgiving people but not of God. A marriage counselor I respect tells me the biggest challenge couples face in restoring a relationship is that one partner will attempt to hold the other partner's mistakes over his or her head as a control device. To restore the relationship, both parties have to forgive and forget. The good news is that God's Word says he forgives us of our sins and remembers it no more. A friend of my mine calls it "divine painting." God takes our black sin stains, paints them with red blood, and makes us white as snow. The Bible is clear, that once forgiven, "God remembers our sins no more."

4. God may forgive and forget, but I can't forgive myself.

This is the core of the problem. This is where a lot of people just lay down or, worse, start digging deeper holes. We will discuss grace that restores, but in a nutshell, this attitude is arrogant and self-destructive. What it really says is, "Jesus's death on the cross wasn't sufficient, and my own opinion of my fall is more important than that of the God who created me and then came and saved me." The attitude that I can't forgive myself, is a complete lack of understanding of the role of grace in our lives, which we will cover in the next chapter. If, the God of perfection and holiness forgives me, I have no choice but to forgive myself in following his example. If, I am going to love my neighbor like myself, I have to learn to love myself. I can't begin to love myself, until I forgive myself.

5. God may forgive me, and I may forgive me, but I can't forget.

There is some truth in this as long as you dwell on the past and not what God has in store for you in the future. I have another friend who took a very hard and public fall—the type of fall that ends careers and causes you to lose friends. If he were evaluated on his lifetime, he would come out well. He is a good person and has done some great things for other people. He and I have discussed how when you're just past getting up from a fall and you're starting to turn the corner, that's when the memories become your enemy. Satan reminds you of your fall and convinces you that everyone knows and everyone has dedicated their every waking moment to talking about you. I am sure God wants to scream, "Get over yourself. You didn't even make eliminations for the Sins Hall of Shame." Most of those selected for the Sins Hall of Shame later became people God called "beloved," "saints," and "apostles," and who went on to do great things for God. The truth is that, at some point, we have to let it go because God has. Others couldn't care less, and it commits you to living in the past. A phrase I repeated over and over again, helped me with the fear that I could never forget all my mistakes. That phrase is, "In Jesus, my past has nothing to do with my future."

6. *If God really forgives me, why am I suffering all these consequences of a forgiven sin?*

We will also deal with this more in the next couple of chapters, but the answer is that falls (sin) have consequences. However, the promise of God is that nothing can separate you from the love of God—nothing. How you approach the consequences will have more to do with how fast and far your comeback becomes through Jesus. Jesus took on the sins of the whole world from all time and marched against all evil, the sins of the world, and still only needed a borrowed, barely used tomb. It will take us longer, sometimes a lifetime, but we will get back to the purpose he created. Remember, God can use anyone and all mistakes, for his glory. More to come.

Do you think if there were any other way for you to be forgiven of your sin and reconnected with our creator, God would have permitted Jesus to suffer and die a cruel death on the cross? Let's not cheapen his sacrifice or water down God's love for us by believing we can't forgive and forget something the God of the universe already has forgiven and forgotten.

CHAPTER 7

GRACE RESTORES

One of my mentors taught me GRACE stands for "God's Riches at Christ's Expense." That's a good way to remember the part of grace that is responsible for saving us—a saving grace. There is a second part of grace, which is a restoring grace. Grace is also "God Restoring at Christ's Expense."

What is the difference between mercy that forgives and grace that restores?

- When Jesus told the thief on the cross he was forgiven, that was mercy. When he told the thief he would be seated next to him in paradise that was grace.
- When the father told the prodigal he could come back into the house that was mercy. When the father said, "Come in not as a worker but as my son," that was grace.
- The paralyzed man whose friends lifted him down through the ceiling was told, "Your sins are forgiven." That was mercy. And now get up, take your mat, and walk. That's grace.

The Greek word *charis* (khar'ece) is most often translated as "grace" (or favor). Depending on the translation, *grace* appears one hundred and fifty or more times in the New Testament. *Charis* comes from the Greek word *chairó*, which is found at least seventy times (again depending on the translation) and means "be glad and to rejoice exceedingly."

Forgiveness covers us with God, our creator. Grace restores us now, in this broken world, and places us back where God intended us to be. Forgiveness is reactive (it forgives something that has already occurred). Grace is proactive. Grace says, "Although I could hold it against you, and, in human terms, would be justified in doing so, let's forget it and move on. Let's, to the extent we can, reverse the damage done and agree to live with what we can't fix without holding it over your head." At some point, grace says, "Let's act like it never happened." Forgiveness focuses on me, the person being forgiven. Grace focuses on Jesus and what he wants to do in my future. Hebrews 4:16 states, "Let us then approach the throne of grace with confidence, so that we may receive mercy and find grace to help us in our time of need."

As we noted, forgiveness is Jesus coming to seek and save the lost. Grace is Jesus coming to give us an abundant life (John 10:10). Forgiveness is because Jesus took our place on the cross for the payment of sins. Grace is that he was resurrected on the third day to prove nothing can stop him, not even death, from loving you.

Why do we have so much trouble accepting grace and therein not getting restored to God's plan for our lives? I think there are a few reasons why accepting restoring grace is so hard, which I'll list. Then we will explore them in detail.

1. God's grace makes no human sense.
2. We don't believe God when he says nothing can separate us from his love.
3. Nothing is free, especially something as good as God's grace.
4. We measure everything on outcomes (our works).
5. We like everything to be about us; grace is about Jesus.
6. We like to control everything; grace requires letting go.
7. We think we are good enough or have paid enough of a price to not need grace.
8. We've made grace a concept and not an experience.
9. Grace causes us to change, and change is scary.

Frederick Buechner wrote:

> The grace of God means something like: Here is your life. You might never have been, but you are because the party wouldn't have been complete without you. Here is the world. Beautiful and terrible things happen. Don't be afraid. I am with you. Nothing can ever separate us. It's for you I created the universe. I love you. There is only one catch. Like any other gift, the gift of grace can be yours only if you reach out and take it. Maybe being able to reach out and take it, is a gift too.

So why don't we reach out and take grace? Why don't we move beyond mercy? Why do we choose to stop at being forgiven?

1. God's grace makes no human sense.

On our own, we would never have come up with grace. It is illogical. It is scandalous. You hurt me, I'll hurt you. An eye for an eye. Show grace to them? I'd rather show them what happens when you mess with me. Being full of grace is not a human behavior. We are taught from a young age that life is about justice. We're taught not to forget those who have wronged us. The idea of getting something we don't deserve seems contrary to "work hard and play by the rules." Grace doesn't make sense from a human perspective, and if you try to accept grace, much less give it away based on your analytical skills, grace will elude you. Grace only makes sense when you see it from God's perspective. A perfect God says that despite all the horrible things you've done, or great things you haven't done, he loves you too much to leave you as you are. Only God could say, "I ignore all the broken promises, lies, and attempts to manipulate me and still love you because you're my creation." To accept grace, we have to move past the illogicalness of grace and trust God when he says, "I so loved you that I gave my only begotten son for you. I love you so much that I want you to have an abundant life. I love you so much, I want you to fulfil the purpose I created you to fulfill."

2. We don't believe God when God says, "Nothing can separate you from my love."

We don't accept and live grace because we change God's meaning. We think, *nothing can separate me from God's love … except for when I cheated, or abandoned my family, or stole, or killed somebody while drunk*, or a hundred other sins we remind ourselves about on a daily basis. We really limit God and cheapen Jesus's death when we add conditions to his forgiveness and grace. His only condition is accepting it. God is a God of second, third, and seventy-times-seventy chances. Nothing can separate us from the love of God, unless we let it. Nothing can separate us unless we choose the "other" rather than the love of God. For some, the "other" is something obviously destructive such as addiction, unfaithfulness, a criminal act or abandonment. However, for some, the "other" is less obvious, working too many hours, being distant from our spouse, pursuit of wealth or recognition when it is substituted for or pursued instead of, the love of God.

3. Nothing is free, especially something as good as God's grace.

We don't accept grace because we want to know the "catch". We are taught that nothing good is free. No one gets something for nothing. There is a cost to a grace that restores. It requires us to give God something he already owns: us. To be fully restored in God's grace, we have to go all-in for Jesus.

God's restoring grace wasn't free. It caused Jesus to leave heaven, come to earth, become a human, and die a horrible and humiliating death on the cross. That's not cheap; that's literally payment in blood. I once heard someone say that my explanation of grace sounded like nothing more than "cheap fire insurance". My response was, it wasn't cheap, it cost Jesus a cruel and miserable death.

4. We measure everything in outcomes (our works).

We don't accept restoring grace because we are used to conditional love and evaluative love. Conditional love is, "I love you if you do something or stop doing something." The love is conditioned on earning it by omission or commission. Evaluative love is when we evaluate the person or ourselves to see how much love, by a human analysis, we deserve. If we do good things (works), we get more love. If we do bad things, we get less love. That makes sense to us, but not to God. The Bible says that while we're sinners, he still loved us. Not because of what we did or didn't do, but in spite of our behavior. Restoring grace can only be accepted when we understand it doesn't make sense; it's just so God. It is similar to how we love babies. The minute you hold your baby, you love him or her. They haven't earned it. In fact, most of what they do initially, doesn't deserve love, but you love them anyway. You love your baby because it is your baby. It is your creation. It is yours to take care of and protect. If, as fallen people we get that concept, how much more does our Heavenly Father who is our creator (and theirs).

5. *We like everything to be about us; grace is about Jesus.*

We don't accept grace because we are obsessed with ourselves. I'm sure God wants to yell down to me sometimes, "Get over yourself." Apparently, in my life, he's assigned that messenger roll to wife. Accepting restoring grace means admitting, it isn't all about me. It isn't about what I've done. Restoring grace requires me to stop focusing on what I did or can do and to focus on what Jesus already did. Restoring grace requires me to focus on God, on his purpose for my life and on bringing praise and glory to him in how I live. There is a massive arrogance in non-believers too. To really believe the whole world exist, solely for me to do whatever I want, regardless of who it hurts and simply for my pleasure requires an incredible ego.

6. *We like to control everything; grace requires letting go.*

Let's be honest: we have control issues—some more than others, but all of us to some extent. We like to decide what we believe, what we do, who we like, and who we spend our time with and our time on. The grace that restores requires us to give it all to God. Note, anything in your life that is more important than your relationship with God, even if, by itself, is good, becomes wrong when it takes God's place. I can promise you, if there is something in your life more important than God, then that is precisely where he will challenge you.

A smart, rich, young ruler came to Jesus. He had kept every commandment (take a deep swallow)—every commandment. Yet, Jesus told him, "You lack one thing". You love wealth and security more than you love God. He walked away. It was too high of a price. We never read about him again in the Bible, but my guess is he hit bottom. To be prodigal, you don't have to be poor; there are plenty of prodigal sons and daughters in the upper One percent. There is solid truth in the advice of the popular gospel song: "Give them all, give them all, give them all to Jesus. Shattered dreams, wounded hearts, and broken toys."

We don't accept restoring grace because, despite the fact that we made a mess of our lives, because we still think we know best. Do yourself a favor: accept restoring grace, give it all to him, and fire yourself as CEO.

7. We think we are good enough or have paid enough of a price to not need grace.

We don't accept restoring grace because—I'll just say it—we're self-righteous. We're self-righteous because despite knowing we have all sinned and fall short, we have created a hierarchy of sin. Remember, a hierarchy of sin is when I say some sins, usually somebody else's sins, are worse than other (usually my) sins. We decide the sins of our neighbors, brothers, sisters, parents, spouses, or church staff are bad sins and our sins aren't that big of deal. We believe the delusion that we've paid the price for our sins on our own or that what we've done is not nearly as bad as what someone else has done. They need grace, not us. I actually had a church member tell me once that she "never sins". That is delusional thinking. I heard a television preacher one time say he only committed "petty sins", now that is a different approach to sin categorization. You cannot earn or work your way to grace. Ephesians 2:8-9 reminds us: "For it is by grace you have been saved, through faith- and this is not from yourselves, it is a gift of God."

8. We've made grace a concept and not an experience.

I meet a lot of people who understand the concept of grace but have clearly never experienced it, at least not experienced it beyond the initial saving grace. Remember, grace has two parts: saving grace and restoring grace. How can you tell they haven't experienced restoring grace? You can tell by their lives. People who have experienced God's restoring grace can't get enough of God. They forget and forgive everyone around them. They love as much as they can love, even when it's risky. They love even when it's not reciprocated or appreciated or wanted. They forgive, give grace, and love even when it's rejected. When you experience restoring grace, it is impossible not to live like someone forgiven and restored. Grace becomes an experience, when it permeates through every aspect of our lives. It becomes an experience when we give away freely mercy that forgives and grace that restores, to every person we meet. Grace, when it goes beyond a concept, to being experienced, leads us to become people known as Christians because of our love, especially for those who our community and unfortunately often the church, consider outcast.

9. Grace causes us to change, and change is scary.

When Jesus walked by a crippled beggar, he asked him, "Do you want to be well?" Strange question? Not really. Jesus was really asking, do you want things to change". Sometimes, I meet people who have fallen, hit bottom, and prefer to stay there. They prefer being miserable to the hard work of submitting to God, asking forgiveness of those they hurt and having to take the shots they will get from the self-righteous grace-deniers. Sometimes, we get used to accepting less than God intended; we forget he intended so much more for us. Not the prodigal son. He decided he had had enough of living with and like the pigs. However, some people will not accept God's restoring grace because they fear the change, God will bring to their life. God does require a genuine commitment to him. The good news is that your best is enough for him. Our inadequacies are enough for him, because Jesus is sufficient. It is work. There is no question, that seeking God and living for him, requires more work than accepting failure, giving up and staying on the bottom. I've never met a person who let God change them, pick them up from the bottom and restore them to the life he has planned for them, who wanted to go back down to the bottom. The first step requires the most faith, but the change he wants to make, is so worthwhile.

CHAPTER 8

THE IMPORTANT DIFFERENCE BETWEEN SELF-DENIAL AND DENIAL OF SELF

In Mark 8:34, Jesus says, "Whoever wants to be my disciple must deny themselves and take up their cross and follow me." To deny yourself means to say no to yourself and yes to God. Here is the problem: for a host of reasons, many of them bad; the church has taught self-denial, rather than denial of self, as a path to Jesus. Jesus wasn't talking about forgoing earthly possessions, not eating certain foods, ignoring the world, etc. One of the mistakes I think we make when we're trying to get back up is we, and a lot of churches, confuse two important concepts. We confuse self-denial with denial of self.

Self-denial is the mentality of creating a list of do's and don'ts and keeping a scorecard of our behavior. It's the mistaken concept of "don't drink, don't smoke, don't dance, and don't date girls who do." The problem with it is it focuses on what you and I can do, and not what God has already done. The other concept that I think is the real focus of restoration is, denial of self. Denial of self is when we submit it all to God. We no longer focus on "I" or "Me," and we focus on him. The focus shifts from what I can do, to what God's already done. The focus is now on my commitment to him, on making him number one in my life. I've had pastors and theological school professors argue with me that I am playing with semantics, that there is no real difference between self-denial and denial of self. They are wrong. I think the distinction is at the heart of the difference between being religious and following Jesus.

Being religious is when we act, do, and say certain things or don't act, do, or say certain things in order to get to God. Following Jesus is when we admit we couldn't, in one hundred years, learn to act in a way that would get us to God. God knows that, so rather than have us struggle our way to him, he sent Jesus and came to us. He came down to our level, because we couldn't get up to his.

COMPARISON OF
SELF-DENIAL V. DENIAL OF SELF

Self-Denial	*Denial of Self*
Focus is on my behavior	Focus in on what Jesus has done for me
Focus is on me controlling	Requires complete surrender to Jesus

Focus is on keeping a list or score	Focus is on my sins being remembered no more
Focus is on avoiding "bad" sins	Focus is on doing the right things under God's direction
Is dependent on my goodness	Acknowledges only God is good
Avoids sin out of fear	Does the right things out of love for Jesus

Even if you could achieve self-denial on your own, it wouldn't, in and of itself, make you a good person, or someone contributing to the kingdom or living a life of joy and abundance. The young ruler came to Jesus, and he had kept all the commandments but walked away unfilled because Jesus requires all of you, not strict obedience to a code of conduct.

Denial of self is when you live the promise of Ephesians 1:11, "In him we were also chosen, having been predestined according to the plan of him who works out everything in conformity with the purpose of his will." In other words, I don't have to accept the awful things I've done or the awful things that have happened to me or those I love. I just have to accept God has a plan and he will make everything work out according to his plan, even all my mistakes.

So what are some of the characteristics of living in denial of self (not self-denial)?

1. I get less important every day. My wants, dreams, and ambitions become his. John 3:30 tells us, "He must become greater; I must become less."

2. The old me is no longer living for me. Galatians 2:20–21 states:

> I have been crucified with Christ and I no longer live, but Christ lives in me. The life I now live in the body, I live by faith in the Son of God, who loved me and gave himself for me. I do not set aside the grace of God, for if righteousness could be gained through the law, Christ died for nothing!

Note, "I do not set aside the grace of God." On our way down, when we hit bottom and when we stay on the bottom, that is what we are doing. We are setting aside the grace of God—God's saving but also restoring grace. That is what grace-deniers attempt to do to you: they attempt to set aside grace, for themselves and especially for you.

3. My focus isn't, not sinning out of fear, but to live a life worthy of Jesus's sacrifice. We won't ever reach worthiness, but we strive to be more Christ-like. Galatians 5:24–25 reminds us, "Those who belong to Christ Jesus have crucified the flesh with its passions and desires. Since we live by the Spirit, keep in step with the Spirit."

4. We quit focusing on the past. The single largest obstacle to becoming all you can become in Christ is dwelling on the past. That's true of people and churches. Ephesians 4:22–24 states:

> You were taught, with regard to your former way of life, to put off your old self, which is being corrupted by its deceitful desires; to be made new in the attitude of your minds; and to put on the new self, created to be like God in true righteousness and holiness.

> Colossians 3:10 says, "And have put on the new self, which is being renewed in knowledge in the image of its Creator." And most familiar and ignored, 2 Corinthians 5:17 says, "Therefore, if anyone is in Christ, the new creation has come: The old has gone, the new is here!"

5. We are willing to pay the price to follow Jesus. The price isn't necessarily to stop or start doing something. Luke 14:27 reminds us, "And whoever does not carry their cross and follow me cannot be my disciple." Luke 9:23–25 says:

> Then he said to them all: 'Whoever wants to be my disciple must deny themselves and take up their cross daily and follow me. For whoever wants to save their life will lose it,

but whoever loses their life for me will save it. What good is it for someone to gain the whole world, and yet lose or forfeit their very self?'

It is likely that at least one cause of your fall was your focus on you and not God … on you and not on others. You and I and countless others have discovered there is no good in gaining the best of the world if we lose our souls on the way. There have been two times in my life that I felt a place I was working at was asking me to lose my soul in pursuit of the world. Both times, what had started as good intentions gradually transformed into greed. I left both places without a job. The first time, there was a job waiting, and I thought, *Great. Following Jesus isn't too costly.* The second time, it took me twenty-three months to find a position three levels down from my former position. Truthfully, we were within months of bankruptcy. It was stressful, hard on our marriage, and, for the first time in my life, I was afraid. It also happened at one of the worst economic times in modern history. I really struggled. It was during this period that I learned to distinguish between the temporary and the eternal.

TEMPORARY THINKING

Either this "Christian thing" is real or it isn't. One contributor to our fall is when we play at faith. If we really believe Jesus is who he says he is, the Son of God and our Savior, then that affects everything in our lives. If we don't believe Jesus is who he says he is, then why give him any consideration at all? Jesus himself eliminated any option of just calling him a good man or teacher or religious leader or prophet.

> "But what about you?" he [Jesus] asked. "Who do you say that I am?" Simon Peter answered, **"You are the Messiah, the Son of the living God."** Jesus replied, "Blessed are you, Simon son of Jonah, for this was not revealed to you by flesh and blood, **but my Father in heaven."** (Matthew 16:15–17)

The importance of who Jesus is and what you believe about him cannot be overstated. If you believe he is the Savior, then everything else, everything, is of secondary importance.

Most of our falls happen because we focus on the immediate and the temporary. In many colleges now, while earning a degree, students create what they call a portfolio. A portfolio is a collection of work from each class, and when taken as a whole, it represents what the students have learned and what they have learned to do, during their education. Universities and employers use a student's portfolio to measure whether or not a student is ready to graduate and has achieved the required outcomes.

We too are building portfolios for our lives. The portfolio doesn't determine our eternity (accepting Jesus does that). The portfolio of our lives reflects what was really important to us in this life, how we spent our time and money, and what our real values were. To be honest, without mercy that forgives and grace that restores, I wouldn't be very proud of my portfolio. That's the great news. Mercy "whites out" all the pages of mistakes and sins. Grace then restores us to recreate the portfolio so that it reflects God's purpose in our lives. It is the ultimate do-over. Temporal thinking means we are focusing only on the immediate and not on the short-term, long-term, and eternal consequences. Temporal thinking asks, "What is it I want now, immediately?" rather than asking the better question, "What should I do now that will help me achieve all that God wants me to achieve?" Temporal thinking leads to bad decision-making. Temporal thinking trades the immediate for the important. It trades temporary enjoyment for sustaining satisfaction. It trades here and now for the eternal.

CHAPTER 9

GETTING BACK UP

FRIDAY, SATURDAY, AND SUNDAY

M ost of us live the Saturday experience. We don't spend much time living in the experience of Friday night's crucifixion or in the Sunday morning resurrection triumph. Most of us spend much of our lives in the Saturday experience, knowing our horrible and awful acts, but having moved beyond them to forgiveness. We don't get to the Sunday resurrection experience because, while we know saving grace, we haven't fully embraced restoring grace—it seems too good to be true.

However, if you've fallen and you're still on the bottom, you absolutely relate to the Friday experience. You relate to living, if it can be called that, a life that is more like the experience of Friday's crucifixion, where Jesus himself wondered, "Father, why did you abandon (forsake) me?" You relate to a life that's dead and buried, with no hope in sight. You'd be thrilled with waiting-out Saturday to see if the resurrection Sunday comes— anything to stop the pain and regret of the fall that led to crucifixion Friday. That is the problem and the temptation. The temptation is to accept God's mercy that forgives and tip your toe into the water of saving grace. But a grace that restores—a resurrected life, especially your life—seems too far.

Have you ever wondered why Jesus was resurrected? It wasn't to save us. His death on the cross paid that debt. We were forgiven and free the minute that Jesus paid the ultimate sacrifice for our sins. Jesus was the necessary sacrificial lamb. The reason for the resurrection was to tell us that not only are we free, not only do we have our lives back, but that God has the power to restore us to what he created us to be. The resurrection was God saying, "If I can overcome death, then there is nothing in your life I can't overcome." The resurrection states that Jesus can resurrect your life from the bad mistakes, tragic lapses in judgment, horrible acts, and wasted years. The resurrection challenges us to believe in not just mercy that forgives, but also in a grace that fully restores. It is a grace that resurrects our lives from the graveyard we created, the grave we dug ourselves, and the last shovel we used to bury ourselves, breathing, but hardly alive.

In the worst period of my life, right when the last shovel was going in the dirt, I did something I had never really done. I asked myself two simple questions: One, what do I really believe? And, two, am I living consistent with those beliefs? For the next several years, I intentionally questioned everything I had always claimed to believe. Some call that a crisis of faith. I call it getting real.

If you know what you believe, and you live according

to what you believe, and what you believe is true, then your circumstances shouldn't have anything to do with how you live or the decisions you make. Let's look at that "getting back up" formula again, more closely.

1. What do I really believe?

For me, the answer is, I believe Jesus Christ is the Son of God. He died on a cross for the forgiveness of my sins, was resurrected to demonstrate his power over everything, and will return someday to take us to eternity (if we don't get there first). I believe he loves me regardless and in-spite of me. I believe he has a plan for my life and eternity. I admit there are issues and beliefs that separate me from others who are also Christians, in the sense I don't believe exactly the same thing, on every issue, that they believe. I disagree with many of them on political priorities. However, as far as the core beliefs I described above, Jesus was born, crucified, and resurrected, and is coming again. I believe it! The more difficult question to answer is next.

2. *Was I living consistent with those beliefs?*

It wasn't difficult to determine the answer that question, but it was to admit the answer to myself. Somewhere along the line, wanting what I want, avoiding conflict, attempting to regain my youth, and measuring success by cultural standards became more important to me, than living what I believed. Let me make it clear that keeping my beliefs, seeking a better lifestyle, supporting a family, and avoiding conflict are not always or automatically, mutually exclusive. Self-denial would suggest you quit pursuing these things. Denial of self teaches you to pursue Jesus and he'll give you what you need, which will become what you want. Psalm 37:3–5 teaches us this principle:

> Trust in the LORD and do good.
> Dwell in the land and enjoy safe pasture.
> Take delight in the LORD,
> **And he will give you the desires of your heart.**
> Commit your way to the LORD.
> Trust in him and he will do this.

Deny yourself and trust him, and he will make sure what's in your heart and what you desire, are the same.

The past five years have been some of the most challenging in my life. As a family, we have faced cancer, a flood, a microburst, and a fire that took our home and all our possessions. Yet, I can tell you that I have found a peace of mind, even in the storms, that only comes from knowing I am right with my creator. To the best of my ability, I am in the center of his will. There have been times when I've made more money, gained more notoriety, and, based on the circumstances of life, have had easier days—but never better days and never more peace. Philippians 4:7, which I call the mental health verse states: "And the peace of God, which transcends all understanding, will guard your hearts and your minds in Christ Jesus." Paraphrased, "when my understanding and everything I observe, tells me I should afraid and worried, God will substitute his peace so that I am neither afraid nor worried."

I encourage you to begin the climb. It won't be easy, but I've found that God will completely change your life in less than a year. If you don't make the change, you will hit bottom again and again. There will be more damage to yourself and those you love, and more time away from what God created you to do. Picture someone trying to make their life better by continuously running their head into a brick wall. It doesn't make any difference how persistent or skilled they are at running head-on into a brick wall, it is still a brick wall. It still damages and hurts them. Picture that same person, taking a step to the right or left and noticing an open door. The answer was there but until they surrendered and were willing to change direction, they were going nowhere. Jesus is the open door.

God stands willing to give you, that which he already paid for through his son Jesus:

- ✓ Mercy that forgives, forgets, and erases all mistakes
- ✓ Grace that saves and grace that restores
- ✓ A lifelong partner and mentor who promises he will never forsake or abandon you

You can learn to live like someone forgiven and who is back among the living.

TALK ABOUT GETTING BACK UP

You may think getting back up is impossible. You may have been down so long, you taste only dirt. Jesus understands. Don't think so? You're wrong. Jesus was 100 percent human when he walked the earth. He was mocked, beaten, lied to, betrayed, falsely accused, tried, convicted, and eventually crucified. In one week, he went from toast of the town, to despised and rejected. Then they killed him: dead, not breathing, all finished.

Yes, your fall was bad. You became emotionally and physically sick. You were a social outcast. Friends abandoned you; family disowned you. It was bad, but you aren't dead. It may have felt like you were crucified, but you are breathing. Jesus died. Jesus was buried. A large stone was rolled in front of his tomb.

But he got back up. He was resurrected. Why? To teach us that it's never over until God says it's over. How? He trusted in an all-powerful, all-knowing Father.

You can do the same. What do you have to lose? You're not going to miss the disgrace or the dirt.

Try praying this:

> God, you are my only hope. It seems to me that I'm down for the count. I'm not dead, but I sometimes feel as if I might as well be. God, I ask you to give me mercy that forgives and grace that restores. I ask you to resurrect me to the person you created me to be. I'll follow if you'll lead. Roll back the stone for me.

THE TRUTH

Either this mercy that forgives and grace that saves and restores is true and, therefore, true for everyone, or it is false for all of us. It isn't true for some and false for others. It isn't a truth for me, but you might find a different truth. It is either real or it is false. I don't know a lot about a lot of things, but I know that mercy forgives and grace restores. I know that because I've personally experienced it. You can too. May I suggest this prayer?

> God, I've made a mess of my life. I don't feel loved or forgiven. I am going to take you at your word when you say you still love me, that you will forgive me, and that your grace is sufficient to restore me to your plan for my life. I am asking you, right now, to forgive me and restore me to who you made me to be. God, please guide me on what to do and the steps to take, and I'll follow. Help me to become confident in your love and forgiveness for me.

If you prayed that prayer and you're sincere, God will forgive you and restore you. You can begin to live like someone forgiven. Author and pastor, Anne Lamott observed, "I do not at all understand the mystery of grace—only that it meets us where we are but does not leave us where it found us."

RELIGION IS NOT WHAT YOU NEED

I have found some religious people in specific, and religion in general, to be counter to the message of mercy and grace. Religion is a human attempt to get to God. Christianity is God coming to us through Jesus. Religion focuses on a list of don'ts. It practices a few rituals and blind obedience to creeds and denominational doctrines. When you hit bottom, the last thing you need is to someone telling you how you don't measure up. You knew that several hundred mistakes ago. Religion is futile; we cannot get to God on our own. It's a cruel joke. It's like putting love, peace, and meaning just beyond our grasp and saying, "Jump. Jump higher, faster, try harder." We still fall short. Religion is about buildings, traditions, hierarchy, and power.

Genuine Christianity is about a person: Jesus. It is based on the belief and our experience that when we bump into Jesus—or, more likely, he causes himself to bump into us—things change. Jesus says, "You're a mess. You tried it on your own and made a mess of your relationships, your career, your talents, and your health, yet, in spite of all that, I love you." Jesus says, "You didn't earn my love, and because of that, you can't lose it." Religion says we *earn* God's love. Christianity says we *accept* God's love. God's love is a gift from God. You can't earn a gift; you can either accept or reject it.

You do not need religion, especially when you are on the bottom. You need Jesus. He is saying, "If you trust me, I can put the mess all back together. I can use all the bad things that happened for your good and for my purpose (Romans 8:28). I can work around the mistakes, the failures, and the disobedience, and still accomplish my plan for you" (Ephesians 1:11).

John Newton was a ship captain who made his wealth in supporting and participating in the slave trade. He was a crude, foul-mouthed man who pursued wealth at all cost. His nickname was the Great Blasphemer. At one point, he sank so low, he was a servant to former slaves. He was on a ship that was nearly destroyed. The wind and waves bashed his ship so badly that most of his crew abandoned the ship, and he had to tie himself to the ship to steer it. John Newton hadn't always been the wreck of a human he was at the time of the storm. He had grown up with a mother who fed and loved him and had taught him the scriptures. As his ship was going down, he called out to God, claiming the promise that Jesus could calm the wind and waves. God showed mercy (forgave him) and grace (saved his life), and he experienced Jesus in a real and genuine way, despite having nothing particularly redeeming to offer God. God rescued him and changed him, not because John Newton deserved it, but because God loved his creation. Just like he loves you and me, regardless of who we have become.

While John Newton was changed on that ship, he didn't change overnight. He actually continued to captain in the slave trade while he began to read his Bible and attended worship when in dock. Over time, he was convicted to give up the slave trade and eventually became a pastor. Eventually, through mercy that forgives and grace that restores, he would leave a wretched and wrecked life behind and write these words:

Amazing grace! How sweet the sound
That saved a wretch like me!
I once was lost, but now am found;
Was blind, but now I see.
'Twas grace that taught my heart to fear,
And grace my fears relieved;
How precious did that grace appear
The hour I first believed.
Through many dangers, toils and snares,
I have already come;
'Tis grace hath brought me safe thus far,
And grace will lead me home …

We've cleaned up the song (which likely was written to the tune of a slave chant) and now sing it in our suits and ties, sometimes with a smug, self-righteous falsehood, that down deep we believe, "We deserved it." Nothing could be further from the truth. However, just because we don't deserve it, doesn't mean it isn't true. Amazing grace, restoring grace, grace that is greater than all your mistakes and mine, is yours, already paid for, you only need to accept it.

CHAPTER 10

A NEW START. WHAT NOW?

I find a lot of comfort in King David. The same man who defeated a giant was considered beloved, a man after God's own heart, and was a great king and leader. He was also narcissistic, inconsistent, an adulterer, a murderer, failed in a cover-up, and created a dysfunctional and rebellious family. He was up and down. David also experienced firsthand, God's mercy that forgives and his grace that restores. You and I can benefit from learning how David was restored.

First, admit your mistakes to God. It is true: he already knows them, and he knows the content of your heart, but there is something powerful in confessing your mistakes and failures to God. Getting things off your chest and acknowledging them to God is the first step to being restored. I made a cross of rocks up on the hill of a place I like to hike. On multiple occasions, I'd hike up that trail and confessed my failures to God, leaving them at the cross.

Second, ask God to forgive you for the mess. David was honest with God and said, "Have mercy on me, O God, according to your unfailing love; according to your great compassion blot out my transgressions" (Psalm 51:1). Notice David didn't blame others, minimize his sins, or try to negotiate terms of his forgiveness. He simply confessed his sins and then asked for forgiveness. If you are trying to minimize your sins or negotiate the terms of your surrender, then you aren't ready to be restored. My guess is you haven't hit bottom yet. Philip Yancey, in his book *Disappointment with God,* observes:

> The people who related to God best--Abraham, Moses, David, Isaiah, Jeremiah--treated him with startling familiarity. They talked to God as if he were sitting in a chair beside them, as one might talk to a counselor, a boss, a parent, or a lover. They treated him like a person.

Third, declare your freedom from your past. There is a reason why the Bible says that in Jesus you are free, free indeed. John 8:36 states, "So if the Son sets you free, you will be free indeed."

Chuck Swindoll, in a daily devotion, noted:

> All who embrace grace become "free indeed." Free from what? Free to walk in the heights without fear. Free from self. Free from shame and condemnation. Free from the tyranny of others' opinions, expectations, and demands. Free to obey. Free to love. Free to forgive others

as well as ourselves. Free to allow others to be whom they are—different. Free to live beyond the limitations of human effort. Free to serve and glorify Christ! Because of grace we have been freed from sin ... from its slavery, its bondage in our attitude, in our urges, and in our actions.

Fourth, take full responsibility for the consequences of your failures.

"For I know my transgressions, and my sin is always before me" (Psalm 51:3–5). This means humbling yourself and asking others to forgive you for the hurt you've caused. You being restored is not dependent on them forgiving you but rather only on you asking. Genuine accountability requires you owning your part of the failures without apportioning a share of responsibility to them.

Fifth, trust God that you are forgiven and that it is forgotten. Remember, your failures were cast as far as the West is from the East and into the depths of the sea, to be remembered no more. Trust God when he says that is what he'll do.

Sixth, start living as someone forgiven. David prayed, "Create in me a pure heart, O God, and renew a steadfast spirit within me" (v. 10) and God did. It is essential you live like you know you're forgiven. This means that when others bring up your fall, you respond with, "You'll be glad to know that I've confessed all my sins to God, and he's forgiven me. He made me a new creation, and I have a new heart, so there is no reason to waste any time talking about the past. If you ask him, he will forgive you too." In Jesus, your past has nothing to do with your future.

Seventh, tell your new story. God can use the biggest mistake you've ever made to show others the way or the way back. David committed to God that if God would restore him, "Then I will teach transgressors your ways, so that sinners will turn back to you. Open my lips, Lord, and my mouth will declare your praise" (vv. 13, 15). You can become a trophy of grace. Remember how you felt when you ran into the grace-deniers or those with the Prodigal's Brother Syndrome? You can be different. You can be one of those people who spread mercy and grace. You can do for someone what you wish someone had done for you. This is your calling, your ministry.

One reason the Apostle Paul was so effective in spreading grace and getting people to move beyond the law, the legalistic attempts to get to God, is that he had been so bound to tradition and the law. Paul was credible because he had been there and done that. You and I are experts on grace because we needed it so much.

Eighth, get over yourself, again. We tend to have the egos to believe God cannot overcome the mistakes in our lives to accomplish his purpose in and for us. The Scripture tells us we're wrong (self-absorbed). "In him we were also chosen, having been predestined according to the plan of him who **works out everything in conformity with the purpose of his will**" (Ephesians 1:11).

God works out everything in conformity with his will. God

takes our mistakes, messes, and sins, and conforms them to his will. You may have considered yourself a world-class sinner; he forgives you, restores you, and conforms all that's happened to his purpose for you.

Ninth, adopt this scripture as your motto for life: "Be joyful in hope, patient in affliction, faithful in prayer" (Romans 12:12). I don't know of any one verse with better advice. Be joyful because you have been forgiven, it has been forgotten, and you have been restored. Be patient in suffering because this life is temporal and the best is yet to come. Be faithful in talking with God and listening to him. He tells us to cast our cares on him because he cares for us. After mercy that forgives and grace that restores, our lives should have hope. We still live in a fallen place, even though we are no longer fallen, so therefore there will be suffering. Staying close to God means staying in contact with God.

Relationship v. Fellowship

Finally, work on the quality of your relationship with God. I have four brothers. One of my brothers is already home. Regardless of the periods we spent lots of time together or times we spent little together, we are and always will be—brothers. That relationship is based on birth. To really enjoy my brothers, I need to spend time with them, talk with them, and work, play, and eat together.

The same is true with you and God. Once you have accepted

his mercy, you have a relationship with him you can't lose. It is a matter of birth: second birth. To really get everything God intended out of the relationship requires spending time with him, talking to him, and working, playing, and eating together.

I found the following steps important in my life, and maybe you will too:

1. **Find a positive church.** One that preaches mercy that forgives and grace that restores. Run from any church that teaches the bad gospel of judgment and condemnation. Philip Yancey, in his book *What's So Amazing About Grace?* States: "I rejected the church for a time because I found so little grace there. I returned because I found grace nowhere else."

2. **Read your Bible.** I know you've heard it before, but there isn't a substitute for knowing what God's love letter to you says.

3. **Surround yourself with people who love you, just for being you.** During my fall, some people said some awful things about me, many of them untrue. My pastor and music and youth leaders in our church told me they loved me. I asked if they wanted to know what was true and what wasn't. All of them and many more stated, "Not really; it wouldn't make any difference. We love you either way—even in spite of yourself." You'll need people like that in your life. Sometimes they are family members, sometimes church family, sometimes friends or co-workers, and, once in a while, even church staff.

But find them. Avoid grace-deniers and those suffering from the Prodigal's Brother Syndrome.

4. **Reach out to others who are fallen.** It is an inconvenient biblical truth, but we are our brothers and sisters' keepers. You will be effective in reaching and helping other fallen people because you've been there. It will also move you occasionally from the ministered to, to the ministering, which is a powerful part of being restored.

5. **Forgive those who have hurt you, abandoned you, and judged you.** As long as you hate them or focus on their treatment of you, you won't be free to be totally restored. Max Lucado is quoted as saying, "Forgiveness is unlocking the door to set someone free and realizing you were the prisoner!"

You are not forgiving them because they were right. You are forgiving them so you can become right. You are forgiving them because we were instructed by God to forgive each other. Peter struggled with forgiving others, and in Matthew 18:21–22, it states, "Then Peter came to Jesus and asked, 'Lord, how many times shall I forgive my brother or sister who sins against me? Up to seven times?' Jesus answered, 'I tell you, not seven times, but seventy-seven times.'"

Jesus wasn't being dramatic; he was making the point that only genuine forgiveness can free us. In Max *Lucado's Inspirational Reader*, he writes:

> You will never forgive anyone more than God has already forgiven you. Is it still hard to consider

the thought of forgiving the one who hurt you? If so, go one more time to the room. Watch Jesus as he goes from disciple to disciple. Can you see him? Can you hear the water splash? Can you hear him shuffle on the floor to the next person? Keep that image. John 13:12 says: "When he had finished washing their feet …" Please note, he finished washing their feet. That means he left no one out. Why is that important? Because that means he washed the feet of Judas. Jesus washed the feet of his betrayer. That's not to say it was easy for Jesus. That's not to say it's easy for you. That IS to say, God will never call you to do what he hasn't already done!

Mercy forgives and grace restores because of who God is and what God already did through Jesus. You are right. You're not worthy of it, neither am I, and good for us for knowing that. But it is still ours to accept.

The two thieves on the left and right of Jesus, when they were all being crucified demonstrate God's love for us. One thief repented, was forgiven (mercy), and was promised a place in paradise (grace). The other thief mocked Jesus, and God loved him enough to not interfere with his freedom of choice. If you are expecting God to make you accept his mercy that forgives and his grace that restores, he won't. Mercy and grace are gifts from God, but like any gift, they have to be accepted.

THE PROBLEM WITH CIRCUMSTANCES

You cannot evaluate God's love by looking at your current circumstances. We live in a fallen place, with fallen people, and really awful things happen. I cannot explain why God permits awful things to happen. I suspect it is because God loves us enough to let us keep our free will, unless we voluntarily surrender it to him. The one thief on the cross continued to reject Jesus, joined in with the Roman soldiers mocking Jesus, and died just as he lived: solely by his own terms. Despite living a life of wrecked relationships, broken dreams, hardship, and continual disappointment, he wouldn't give it all to Jesus, even at death. God loved that thief by permitting him to do it his way, even if his way led to death. Make no mistake, that thief, who rejected Jesus paid the ultimate cost for his rejection, nonetheless God loved him until his last breath. The other thief, who had lived an equally awful life and like you and I had done nothing to earn it, accepted God's gift of Jesus and ended up in paradise.

Evaluating God's love for you by your current circumstances is a recipe for failure and disaster. We should evaluate God's love for us by his Word. We will not understand everything that happens in our lives until heaven, and then I am not sure it will matter all that much to us. While Jesus was dying on the cross, he did not evaluate his Father's love for him by his current circumstances. His circumstances were awful. Jesus had been beaten and mocked, flogged, nailed to a cross, and pierced with a spear while wearing a crown of thorns that had been pressed into his head. He felt forsaken (he said so). However, rather than deciding his Father didn't love him, he surrendered to God's will. He didn't evaluate God's love for him by analyzing his circumstances, and neither should we. God's Word tells us:

For God **so** loved the world, that he gave his only Son, that whoever believes in him should not perish but have eternal life. (John 3:16)

But God shows his love for us in that **while we were still sinners,** Christ died for us. (Romans 5:8)

Your circumstances do not define you; God does. Neither the valley nor the mountaintop experience defines us; God does. Neither being on top nor hitting the bottom defines us; God does. This concept is so important because if you assess your relationship with God, on your circumstances, you will miss the point. God loves you; you didn't earn it, and *you can't lose his love.* He loves you on your best day, your worst day, and all the other days too. He loves you when you're faithful and when you fall. Circumstances are sometimes the result of our choices while living in a fallen world, and sometimes just the outcome of living in a fallen world, regardless of our circumstances, they don't define us.

Getting Up Is So Day-to-Day

The hardest part of getting back up is that it is so day-to-day. There are no quick fixes or solutions. God's mercy that forgives and grace that restores starts the minute we accept it. However, giving it all to Jesus, learning to follow him, developing a trust that his way is the best way and that his way is built on his love for us, is a daily event. Actually, it's a minute by minute, thought by thought, and decision by decision. Galatians 2:20 states:

> I have been crucified with Christ and I no longer live, but Christ lives in me. The life I now live in the body, I live by faith in the Son of God, who loved me and gave himself for me.

It means every day, with every choice, I am crucified with Christ. I am no longer living for my own whims and wants but rather by "faith in the Son of God." I live by faith in Jesus, whom I know (despite my circumstances) is faithful and trustworthy. I know he is trustworthy because he "loved me and gave himself for me." I didn't earn his love and, therefore, can't lose it. We choose to surrender to him and live for him because we love him. Get back up; you're loved. God isn't finished with you.

ABOUT THE AUTHOR

Pastor Dr. David Harpool is the senior pastor of First American Baptist Church Longmont, Colorado. He earned a PhD in Higher Education Leadership with Distinction from Saint Louis University, a Juris-Doctorate from the University of Missouri-Hulston School of Law, where he served as student-body president. He earned a Bachelor of Science in Education from Missouri State, where he was selected the Sysscliff Outstanding Education Major. Dr. Harpool attended Iliff Seminary in Denver, Colorado.

Dr. Harpool has served on staff at Ridgecrest Baptist Church, South Haven Baptist Church, First Presbyterian-Columbia, and other churches in the Midwest. He has served as president of three colleges and universities. Dr. Harpool was a state debate champion and public speaker in high school and college, and finished third in the National Cross-Examination Debate Association Collegiate Tournament.

Dr. Harpool is married with three children and lives in Boulder, Colorado.

CHAPTER NOTES AND DISCUSSION QUESTIONS

Chapter 1: Mercy and Grace are for Messes

1. Have you ever caused or been a real mess?
2. Why do you think Jesus spent so much time with the messes of his day?
3. Why would a perfect God send Jesus to rescue such imperfect people?
4. What does *mercy* mean?
5. What does *grace* mean?
6. What is the difference between mercy and grace?
7. Why do some churches spend so much time talking about what the Bible says so little about and so little time talking about what the Bible says so much about— love, mercy, grace?

Chapter 2: Here in the Real World, People Fall

1. Can you think of someone who was once close to Jesus but had a fall and now is distant? Pray for them, right now.
2. Why does the Church "kill" its wounded?
3. Why do you think we fall?
4. Why do you think we turn away from Jesus just before and right after a fall, when we need him the most?

Chapter 3: How Falls Happen

1. Review the steps of a fall. Do you think they accurately describe a fall?
2. Have you ever taken any or all of the steps of a fall?
3. Why is "fall from grace" inaccurate to describe what God is willing to do for us?
4. What is the evidence in someone's life when they fall?
5. What does it mean to you when we say someone has "hit the bottom"?
6. Who are some of the people in the Bible who took a fall?

Chapter 4: Exactly What We Didn't Need

1. What are the characteristics of someone who suffers from the Prodigal Brother Syndrome?
2. What are the characteristics of a bottom-feeder?
3. Why do you think it is so hard for some people to give mercy?
4. Why do you think it is so hard for some people to give grace?
5. Does someone have to experience grace to be able to give it?
6. What is the connection between saving grace and restoring grace?

Chapter 5: Stopping the Storm Cycle; Finding Shelter

1. How can we be a shelter for someone in the midst of a storm?
2. How does a crisis affect your perspective?
3. Why do we become fearful in a crisis?
4. Is the belief that "I am too far away from God to get back" evidence of reality or a faith problem?
5. What would make a church welcoming to someone in the midst of a storm?
6. Why was Jesus asleep when the storm hit the boat?
7. Why did the disciples not think Jesus cared during the storm?

Chapter 6: Forgiveness (Mercy): the First Step on the Path to Standing Up

1. What does God do with our sin?
2. Does God remember our sins?
3. What is the difference between mercy and justice?
4. What are examples of God's mercy from the Bible?
5. How do you and I show mercy?
6. When was an example of your church showing mercy?
7. What is an example of you showing mercy?
8. When was a time when you received mercy from God?

Chapter 7: Grace Restores

1. What is a good way to explain saving grace?
2. What is a good way to explain restoring grace?
3. What is grace so hard to give?
4. When is a time when you gave grace to someone?
5. When is a time when you received grace from God?
6. Is any mistake or sin or fall, other than rejecting Jesus, beyond God's grace?

Chapter 8: The Important Difference between Self-Denial and Denial of Self

1. What is the difference between self-denial and denial of self?
2. Which concept self-denial or denial of self, does religion, in general, teach?
3. Which concept of self-denial or denial of self does your church teach?
4. Which concept of self-denial or denial of self, did Jesus live and teach?
5. Which concept of self-denial or denial of self, do you live?
6. Why is it easier to live self-denial than true denial of self?

Chapter 9: Getting Up

1. What is the Friday night of the crucifixion experience?
2. Have you ever felt like you were in a Friday night experience?
3. What does it mean when we say that we live most days in the Saturday of the crucifixion experience?
4. Why are we stuck in the Saturday of the crucifixion experience?
5. When have you experienced Resurrection Sunday?
6. What keeps us from experiencing Resurrection Sunday?
7. What does the level of our belief and faith have to do with whether our experience is more like Friday, Saturday, or Sunday of the crucifixion and resurrection experience?

Chapter 10: A New Start. What Now?

1. Have you asked for forgiveness of your sins?
2. What is the danger of an unconfessed sin?
3. Have you accepted God's saving grace?
4. Have you accepted God's restoring grace?
5. What do you think God thinks of you?
6. Why is reading the Bible important to accepting mercy that forgives and grace that restores?
7. Do you know God is not mad at you?
8. Do you know God loves you?
9. Have you ever notice that John 3:16 says, "For God *so* loved …"

Made in the USA
Monee, IL
01 November 2019